Intuition Unlocked

Discover Your Superpower
Speak the Language of the Universe

Cielo C. Canlas

First published by Ultimate World Publishing 2021
Copyright © 2021 Cielo Canlas

ISBN

Paperback: 978-1-922597-31-1
Ebook: 978-1-922597-32-8

Cover design: Ultimate World Publishing
Layout and typesetting: Ultimate World Publishing
Editor: Rebecca Low
Cover Photo: Paul Smith

Ultimate World Publishing
Diamond Creek,
Victoria Australia 3089
www.writeabook.com.au

Testimonials

"Very intriguing, to say the least! I have to admit, I'm not much of a reader, at least not for pleasure; however, I could not stop reading it once I started!"
~ Dr. Glenn T. Poulain, Chiropractic Physician

"Compelling read which gives insight into the power of your subconscious mind! Fascinating stuff!"
~ Valeska Pawlak, Media Relations

"Chills. Straights chills. The mere idea that we exist as a soul but have possibly lived our entire lives as a body, not connected with our true self, is thought-provoking! This is a must-read, even if you aren't sure you are ready for how your life may be changed!"
~ Michelle Thome-Kaufman, BSW, MSW

Dedication

This book is dedicated to my former self.
Thank you for doing the painful work.
Remember when you were looking
for the light at the end of the tunnel?
It was YOU!

Hindsight + insight + foresight = God's Light.

I would also like to dedicate this book to my daughter Cassidy Rae, my heart. She is a product of my journey, as she was only 12 years old when my spiritual awakening began. She has experienced tremendous pain and suffering through my brokenness. If there is anything I could change in my life and in my journey, it would only be that. Kaz, you are, by far, the most important thing to me. I never knew I could love something or someone so much until I had you. You inspired and motivated me to become the best mom I could be because I knew you deserved better. In fact, you deserve the world.

Words cannot express how very proud I am of the beautiful woman you have become: intelligent, empowered, and a humanitarian who advocates for social injustices and meaningful issues. The world is yours to conquer, and more importantly, intuit. May you always be Divinely guided and may the generational trauma we all carry in our family lineage stop with you.

I love you times a thousand and... ____!

Contents

Preface

I came into this world an empath, not knowing or understanding why I had such deep, profound feelings and emotions, and the ability to pick up the same of those around me.

This beautiful gift is often viewed as both a blessing and a curse, because, on one hand, you can truly understand others to the depths of their souls, sometimes more than they can understand themselves. On the other hand, you can truly "feel" others to the depths of their souls, often taking on their emotions as if they were your own. Unfortunately, empaths do not come into this world with a manual on how to manage their gifts. We figure it out by trial and error, and often, those errors can have a detrimental impact on our mental, emotional, and physical health over time.

As I got older, I learned through the hardest of life lessons that I had to manage my sensitive nature instead of allowing it to manage me, or better yet, control me! Imagine walking around like a lint-roller, picking up emotions and energy all around you—it was absolutely draining and overwhelming. I was clueless it was happening. All I knew was that when I was around certain people, places, or situations, I would feel exhausted and sometimes even ill.

I would find myself lying in bed for days at a time. It wasn't until my gift of intuition opened up that I realized there was something more to learn and explore. That led to years of seeking, and as God promised, I found. My gifts continued to evolve and develop, and I learned not only to master my gift of empathy but my gift of intuition as well. They naturally went hand in hand, and a whole new beautiful world opened up to me filled with Divine blessings and guidance.

Up until that point, I had always worked in the human services field; in fact, it is what I had originally majored in during college. I worked as a counselor, advisor, teacher, case manager, and recovery care coordinator. Never realizing in all those jobs I was naturally led or guided to use my God-given gifts. Fast-forward to today, I have my own business and practice, "Island Intuitive", where I provide spiritual advising, mentoring, teaching, and healing to clients from all around the world.

In my spiritual journey, I have learned that we are a soul, first and foremost, and we all have the gift of intuition. It is so much more than what people think it is or define it as, this "gut feeling or hunch". It is not that simple. In fact, it is quite complex. It is also quite profound, meaningful, and spiritual. We are all meant to experience this life-changing, transformational journey, and it is not by accident or coincidence that this book is in your hands right now. Nor was it a coincidence or an accident that I authored this very book. The writing of this book, this very topic, was not "planned". Heck, writing ANY book was not planned. I didn't seek it out; rather, it sought me—at just the right time, at just the right place, under just the right circumstances. I have learned that when a door supernaturally opens, you simply step through—without second-guessing it, without having all the answers of who, what, when, where, why, and how and definitely without allowing fear to stop you.

My hope and prayer is that after you finish reading this book, you will have a new lens through which you view yourself, the world around you, and all that exists beyond your physical eyes. Your intuition is the gateway and connection to Higher realms, including your Highest Self. Let the ascending begin!

Introduction

The journey to unlocking my intuition started in 2012. My marriage of over 17 years had ended in divorce, and I was truly broken and lost. Truth be told, I was lost long before then and merely a fragment of my former myself. In fact, I didn't even know who that former self was. My identity had revolved around being a military spouse and living this very transitionary lifestyle for so long. My identity was also wrapped up in being a mother and a dog mom. Much of my personal goals over the years either had to be put on hold or given up altogether with the lack of stability the military lifestyle brings. When I was finally able to focus on myself, it still wasn't easy: working full-time, going to school full-time, being a full-time mom, living away from family or any true support system, and having a husband who had to deploy and leave us for months at a time. Half my life had passed by, and I wasn't living. I was existing, and in some sense, surviving.

So, I found myself single again at the age of 44, yet another major life transition. You'd think that with all the transitions the military lifestyle brought me in over 17 years that I would be a pro by now. Although I did develop some level of resiliency over the years, this transition was very different. This, in fact, would be the first time in my life I had to go at it alone. There were so many things I had to learn about life. Unfortunately, being a spouse in the military kind of lends itself to becoming dependent. It was a scary time in my life filled with uncertainty, tears, anger, confusion, resentment, and the lowest of all lows. The obstacles and struggles came one right after another. I got into several car accidents, totaling two cars in one year. My job had enforced salary cuts by 25%. The tenants in my rental home had informed me there were busted pipes and the bathroom floors and carpet had been flooded. My old, sweet, little dog lost her eyesight and began showing dementia symptoms. My daughter was in the middle of puberty and going through her own changes, and I was experiencing my own health challenges, likely due to the significant, compiling stress I was under. My entire foundation: home, finances, relationships, job security, health, and sense of self had been tattered and tested to its limits.

This series of occurrences of "life falling apart" went on for another two to three years. I remember begging God to please let me come up for air. I literally felt like I was drowning. I was exhausted. It felt like my heart and soul were being excavated, the valley of the shadow of death. Little did I know at the time that I was going through a "Spiritual Awakening". I had no idea what that even was. I had been experiencing the "Dark Night of the Soul", as it were. A rite of passage...the breakdown to break-through! I wasn't familiar with any of this. All I knew was that my faith was somehow getting me through...barely. Towards the end, I kept believing that all of this suffering wouldn't go in vain. That this would be used mightily one day, and I stood on His word: Jeremiah 29:11, Romans 8:28, Psalm 34:18, Deuteronomy 31:8, and I could go on and on. In the process of trying to find myself again, I instead learned the truth of who I was: a spiritual being having a human experience, and found a whole new world open up to me. This was a healing journey, and the best was yet to come.

As I was waiting for my divorce to be finalized, I began dating again. I say "again", but what I really mean is "for the first time". I wasn't ever really the dating type. I took relationships very seriously, and I preferred to be in a committed relationship. Nonetheless, as most women do when they are newly single, I had a bunch of girlfriends rooting for me to put myself out there again, and in some cases, they even lived vicariously through me! God, I love my girlfriends! So, there I was on match.com with a profile that consisted of an about me write-up, followed by my interests, what I was looking for, and a handful of pictures that surprisingly flattered even my own ego. Ha! ha! Well, I must say that match.com was definitely an ego-boost. After having been married for so long, you wonder if people would really find you attractive anymore, so when you get those eager messages in your inbox, it kind of feels like when you're back in middle school or high school and feeling awkward around a crush. After a short time, I finally got the hang of it, and it turned out to be pretty fun. It was nice to have another "adult" to talk to. Well...in most cases, anyway. So, off I went on dates for coffee, dinner, drinks, dancing, hikes, and museums, and it was the perfect distraction from my chaotic life.

As I mentioned earlier, at the time, I didn't know this was a healing journey I was on. As it turns out, relationships serve as our biggest mirrors, reflecting back to us what we need to heal within, and I was about to find out in a big way. As faith would have it, I went on a business trip to San Diego for job-related training. Little did I know, my spiritual world was about to be turned upside down, as if it wasn't enough that my physical world was still recovering from being in shambles. On day two of training, my phone alarm rang at 6 a.m., and as I grabbed it to turn it off, I saw a message pop up from my email, informing me that my divorce had been finalized that day. It was this bitter-sweet feeling. I laid in bed and grabbed my morning prayer book, read it, and then placed it on top of my heart. I cried for a bit, yet in that moment, I knew I was really going to be ok. It was a new day, and His mercies were new.

I got dressed, grabbed my work bag, and made my way downstairs to our training. I walked in and noticed there were a bunch of other people sitting in the training with us, uniformed Marines. I made my way to my table on the other side of the room, but when I got to my seat, a Marine was sitting there. I scanned the surrounding tables for a place to sit and just then he said, "Oh I'm sorry. Is this your seat?" Or something to that effect; honestly, I don't remember what he said, but what I do remember and will never forget is what happened when we locked eyes.

In those few seconds, he looked at me in such a way as if he looked right through my soul, and I believe he had. His eyes locked onto mine in a state of amazement, confusion, surprise, and his energy channeled into mine as well. Something about it felt intense and familiar, yet confusing all at the same time. I made my way to the next table, and I continued to feel his eyes discreetly locked on to me. Throughout the training, I could energetically feel his presence focused on me. During the break, we exchanged a few words and every time he looked into my eyes, it's as if he saw a ghost. It was like something out of a movie, very surreal. I couldn't quite pinpoint what it was, but I knew it was something I had never experienced before. I continued to try to brush it off until the training broke for lunch.

My girlfriend and I left for lunch and took her car out, looking for a place to grab food quickly. We stopped by at least three places, and they were all too busy with our limited time, so with only about 25 minutes left at that point, we made our way to this Mexican restaurant. As we walked up to the entrance, guess who was sitting outside having lunch with his co-workers? Yup, that same guy! We chuckled and waved hi as I made my way inside, ordered and sat down. A few minutes later, he came in to refill his drink, even though it was still clearly topped off. He continued to chat some more before heading back to training. All the while, every time our eyes locked, it was still that intense, indescribable feeling of this guy looking right through me, but not in a bad way.

Returning from lunch, they broke us up into groups. Yup, you guessed it. He was in my group. I awkwardly kept my gaze away from him as he gestured to share his worksheet with me. I smiled and gestured I was good. When the training ended, a group of us decided we would grab a cocktail at the bar down the hall. We proceeded to say goodbye to each other and said, "Nice to meet you," when all of a sudden, he and his friend decided to join us for a couple of drinks. (You know, to let traffic die down before they head out. Wink-wink!) The whole group ordered drinks and the next thing we knew, we were in our own little world off to the side. We talked for three hours straight. The conversation just flowed, laughter ensued, and we learned that we had a similar history in terms of going through a divorce (mine just finalized that day, and he was still in the midst of his). It was just comfortable, familiar, and easy. It was time to leave, and we gave each other a quick hug goodbye and walked away...and at just the right moment, we both looked back at each other simultaneously, scratching our heads, wondering what the heck just happened. For those of you reading this who have experienced a soul connection before, you will totally get it. It's one of those things that, until you've experienced it, there are no words that can do it justice.

It wasn't about attraction, it wasn't about lust, it wasn't about anything we can humanly understand or reference about love and relationships. It was nothing short of...spiritual. As if our three-hour conversation at the bar wasn't long enough, he texted and called me again when he got home, and I got back to my room. We proceeded to talk for another two hours, but this time, the conversation focused around, "What is this? What the heck is this?!" We saw each other one more time a day later before I had to fly back to Hawaii. After our brief meet-up for a quick drink, he walked me back to my rental car, we locked eyes to say goodbye, and we both simultaneously leaned in to kiss each other goodbye. That kiss...I don't even know what to say about it. Again, it was nothing short of Divinely orchestrated. It was unlike any other kiss we ever experienced before, and in fact, scared the bejesus out of both of us. Out of breath, I quickly hopped in my car without uttering a word and nervously screeched out of the parking lot like a bat out of hell. He stood there in shock and nearly got ran over. With my heart pumping and racing, I safely got back to my hotel room and was replaying everything in my mind. I remember asking God, "What was THAT?!"

What that was, was, a jolt to the soul—the portal opening up to the spiritual world and from that day forward, I/we would experience things that did not make any logical sense and couldn't be chalked up to mere coincidence. We were somehow spiritually connected. It scared us both half to death at times. It's like we were magnetically pulled towards each other spiritually, but our physical, human self was absolutely confused and terrified of this connection. It didn't make logical sense and didn't match any of our previous experiences for reference. We felt like we had known each other for a lifetime. Our thoughts were synchronized. We'd text each other at the exact same time or say the exact same things. We would pick up on each other's energy and know what the other was feeling. We could sense things. It was this absolutely, crazy phenomenon. It was like a vacuum that kept sucking us in, even when we would try to fight it.

We started seeing all kinds of blatant signs and symbols in our external environment: the clocks would always show us when it was 11:11 a.m. or p.m. We experienced a series of unexplainable things. For example, one time we met up in Vegas, and we were standing next to each other outside the Bellagio waiting for the dancing fountain waters to start. Our elbows were resting on the guard rail, and the tops of our shoulders slightly touched. Immediately, we felt a buzzing, vibrating sound that made us both flinch back. I thought he had his phone in his hand or in his shirt pocket, but he didn't. It was in his other pant pocket and there was no evidence of any missed call, alarm, or anything that would make it buzz. Besides, we both felt it directly on our arms, the parts that touched each other. It felt like an electric shaver. He turned pale and felt like he was going to pass out. We had to sit him down somewhere inside the lobby while I searched everywhere for bottled water. We were literally stunned and sat there quietly, not talking about it.

Another time, he had texted me, "Hello?" I joked and started texting him the next line in the lyrics from the song "Hello" by Lionel Richie. We went back and forth trading off lines and chuckled about it. When I got to work a couple of hours later, I suddenly heard the front office playing music, which never happens. I work for the Marine Corps, and they don't just have random music playing out loud out of nowhere in the middle of a workday, especially not Lionel Richie! I leaned in and heard the infamous first keys of the song and then the distinct lyrics. I was in the middle of working, and it stopped me in my tracks. I texted him and said, "You are NOT going to believe this!!" To which he replied, "It's playing isn't it?" (mic drop!) What?! How could this be?

Those are just a few examples of the multiple synchronicities, as they are called. It was an undeniable connection, and this relationship would eventually mirror all the parts of myself I had yet to heal. It was the impetus of a very special, spiritual, yet painful and difficult long-distance relationship. I had only ever seen him twice in the one and a half years we dated, yet I never felt closer and more connected to anyone at the time, despite the distance. This relationship would stretch me so far outside my comfort zone and magnify every nook and cranny of my being...all for the sole purpose (and soul purpose) of exponential growth, healing, and transformation. In fact, we are all called to do this inner-work, this inner-healing, to bring awareness to our human brokenness and unconscious fragmented pieces. My past heartbreaks were my breakthroughs; my tests turned into my testimonies. This was the portal in which the language of the Universe first reached me. It is my hope that this book serves the same purpose for you.

"Intuition Unlocked" takes you on a spiritual journey, yet it is so much more than what you might expect. Filled with a combination of hard scientific evidence, psychological principles, the controversies and inner struggles related to religious beliefs, and first-hand accounts from my own journey and my clients', you'll begin this book by understanding the most basic definition of what intuition is. But equally, if not more importantly, we discuss what it definitely is not. The chapters delve deep into our subconscious mind, which I refer to as the imposter, who is running the show in our lives. How this powerful part of our mind can wreak havoc in ways that we don't even realize. In addition to the imposter, we must also be aware of the comp**YOU**ter within. That is, all the childhood programming we have and carry into our adult selves. We begin to understand where our beliefs and perceptions come from and bring awareness to any biases we hold so we can distinguish all the key parts of ourselves. If we don't fully know who we are, we can't recognize which voice speaks to us, which voice we should be listening to, and why.

The chapters continue to unfold, focusing on the mind and in fact, asking you to, "Mind your busyness" – the distractions of our everyday life that prevent us from accessing this intuitive mind of ours. I discuss the scientific evidence of mindfulness and meditation and share some practical techniques to strengthen our mind like a muscle. We stay *right* on track by discussing the right brain hemisphere where our intuitive mind resides and how we can nurture this side of our often neglected minds. Next, we will focus on "Soul Goals" and why our soul-self should be at the forefront running the show, instead of our humanly egoic self. We will compare the characteristics between our ego and our soul to clearly ascertain the differences. The soul is the goal. We finally "Come to our Senses" by exploring our five senses and beyond, realizing our intuition is not limited to just these five. We explore the energetic layers of our body and the energy all around us. We delve into the spiritual gifts of the "Clairs", which expands our knowledge of the five senses as we know them and try some practical exercises to bring awareness to which may be your natural abilities and how to develop them all. I help you recognize the language of the Universe, in signs and symbols, otherwise known as synchronicities. Things we may "see" in our everyday lives but don't fully capture and experience the magic of. Lastly, we tie it all together in how this all unlocks your intuition and catapults your healing within.

This little book helps us open our spiritual eyes and mind while simultaneously letting go of aspects of ourselves that no longer serve us. What is taught cannot be untaught and will truly expand your consciousness of the world around you like never before—a Spiritual Awakening, minus all the heartache. I took one for the team! Enjoy!

Your Superpower

Have you ever used a navigation system while driving your car, such as Google Maps or a GPS, to prevent you from getting lost? Or perhaps you used it to get from point A to point B using the fastest route to avoid traffic, accidents, or construction along the way. Or maybe you've gone as far as downloading that app on your phone that alerts you of cops hiding out, ready to slap you with a speeding ticket as you zip on by. If you're the latter, this is a judgment-free zone, just arrive alive, please!

Well, I must admit, I am guilty of using Google Maps pretty much every time I drive, even to the places I frequent. My friends make fun of me for this, but I can't help it! I tend to daydream when I drive, so I like having the reassurance of that voice telling me where to turn, when to turn, or to offer me a different route. I absolutely hate getting lost. That sinking feeling when you realize you've taken the wrong highway or exit and end up in some unfamiliar, remote, sketchy place. You slow down and start ducking your head, squinting, and attempting to read the road signs. Meanwhile, cars behind you are irritated, on your tail, honking or passing you and giving you dirty looks. You fumble around, reaching for your glasses and your cell phone, so you can call to let them know you're lost and late, but no one answers. So, you continue driving, going round and round, feeling more stressed with each passing minute. You don't know where the heck you are, nothing looks familiar, you don't know which direction to go, you glance at your gas tank to ensure you have enough gas, you check to see if you have enough charge on your phone, you start reliving every horror movie you ever saw on Netflix, you ensure your doors are locked, your sweaty hands grasping the steering wheel...Just me on the last three? Ummm...Ok. But you get the gist of what I'm saying. No one likes to be lost. No one likes to "guess" which road they should take. No one likes to feel stuck in the middle of nowhere. No one likes to feel uncertain and scared. No one likes to feel out of control, whether that's on the road, in life, or in general.

Well, long before all this technology was ever built into your car or phone to make driving easier for you, you had an internal navigation system to make life easier for you too. It is called your intuition, and it is the compass of your soul. Its capabilities far exceed anything in the market today, it is smarter than any smartphone, it's absolutely free (and priceless at that). Yet still, not everyone uses it or uses it to its full capacity, anyway. But why wouldn't you? Like the scenario above, wouldn't you rather avoid getting lost, avoid any unnecessary delays or dangers in your path, and instead take the clear, unobstructed route to eliminate uncertainty, fear and anxiety in your life's journey?

"We are born with this inner guidance, which comes in the form of the emotions and desires that lead us toward things (including

thoughts) that feel good and are good for us, and away from things that feel bad and are bad for us" (Northrop, 2020). Our intuition is an innate part of who we are. It is our Superpower, our sixth sense, our inner voice. Our intuition gives us this knowing, instinctive feeling. This immediate understanding of people, situations, events, and places, without any logical reasoning or proof. It gives us answers in the midst of confusion or indecision. It gives us the confidence to discern what is best for us. It teaches us to trust and submit.

As an Intuitive Empath with a Spiritual Advising and Coaching practice, I have had hundreds of clients who come to me for guidance, especially in times of struggle. They may have a dire problem they are seeking answers to and feel confused about which direction to go, whether it be about love and relationships, career and life purpose, money and finances, or their own spiritual journey. Many are in emotional distress or mental turmoil. Their minds filled with questions, their hearts heavy, seeking answers. Using my gift of intuition, which I have developed and mastered over the years, I can quickly tune into their situation by seeing, sensing, feeling, and knowing the truth and dynamics behind it and guiding them through any unseen, underlying or unconscious issues or obstacles. This allows them to find clarity and direction, leaving them feeling assured, reassured and at peace. I consider my work to be extremely sacred. My intuition and wisdom are channeled through my Divine connection, using my Higher Self, Holy Spirit. It is always such a beautiful and powerful experience to help others in this way. They start off stressed and leave our session feeling blessed. I must confess, I feel equally blessed by them and the work that I do.

One of the things that's important to me when working with clients is that they leave feeling empowered and filled with faith. Not only about their situation, but about who they are as a spiritual being with the gift of intuition themselves. We are not just merely this human body, this physical human form. We all have this Superpower, this inner compass, to navigate this lifetime with. What stands in the way of people fully stepping into it is doubt, fear and uncertainty. Some people doubt their own intuitive abilities even exist and tend to chalk it up to coincidence. A common example of this is when someone suddenly pops into your mind one day, maybe someone you haven't seen or spoken to in a long time. You wonder how they're doing and have some fleeting thoughts about them. Perhaps you even intend to reach out, but life gets busy, and you never get around to it. Then, lo and behold, not long after, that person reaches out to you via text, phone call or DM on your social media saying you've popped into their mind and they just wanted to say hi and see how you're doing. Or maybe they're going through a rough patch in their life, and you picked up on their energy because of it.

This is a simple example of something that happens fairly frequently, yet people won't attribute that to intuition. They'll call it a coincidence. Other reasons people may not step into their intuition is because of fear: fear of the unknown, fear of what they'll experience or fear that it goes against their beliefs or religion. They may consider it "witchy", "woo-woo", "psychic" or even "demonic". The truth of the matter is, intuition is a natural part of who we are. Just like we have our five senses, intuition can be considered somewhat of an extension of that, thus the coined term "sixth sense"; however, it requires a deeper level of receiving, understanding and processing of information. Perhaps some people are averse to the notion of intuition because it cannot be measured or quantified, and people tend to be more comfortable believing in things they can substantiate or logically understand. Unfortunately, things in the spiritual world rarely work that way.

If you are religious and feel fear or uncertainty around this subject, I can assure you that tapping into your intuition is not evil, but is, in fact, a blessing. I am living proof. Intuition and being intuitive, as I consider myself, is not being a "psychic, fortune-teller, soothsayer, witch or sorcerer". Although, just for clarification and educational purposes, I feel compelled to explain something so widely misunderstood and that is the actual meaning and definition of the word "psychic".

Merriam-Webster dictionary defines the word psychic as:

1: *of or relating to the psyche (the human soul, mind, or spirit)*

2: *lying outside the sphere of physical science or knowledge: immaterial, moral, or spiritual in origin or force.*

3: *sensitive to nonphysical or supernatural forces and influences: marked by extraordinary or mysterious sensitivity, perception, or understanding.*

4: *Supernatural forces meaning of or relating to an order of existence beyond the visible, observable Universe; especially; of or relating to God.*

Dictionary.com defines psychic similarly:

1: *of or relating to the human soul or mind; mental (opposed to physical)*

2: *psychology. pertaining to or noting mental phenomena.*

3: *outside of natural or scientific knowledge; spiritual.*

4: *of or relating to some apparently nonphysical force or agency*

5: *sensitive to influences or forces of a nonphysical or supernatural nature*

Lastly, Wikipedia:

> *The word "psychic" is derived from the Greek word psychikos ("of the mind" or "mental") and refers in part to the human mind or psyche. The Greek word also means "soul". The word derivation of the Latin psȳchē is from the Greek psȳchḗ, literally "breath", derivative of psȳchein, to breathe or to blow (hence, to live).*

> *A person who claims to use extrasensory perception (ESP) to identify information hidden from the normal senses.*

The word "psychic" has been so misused and misrepresented that it now carries a negative connotation to some people, and there is a preconceived idea of what it is, much like the words "car salesman or used car salesman". Unfortunately, psychic abilities and fortune-telling have been used interchangeably and promoted as such, sometimes even within the community, that to the layperson, it brings about images of a mysterious woman with a scarf headdress, big hoop earrings, layers of clothing and a long skirt, dark red lipstick, long black nails, with a crystal ball on top of a table full of candles, funky incense, a ouija board and a black cat with an arched back behind her. Whew! I got chills typing and reading that! For this reason, I do not like to associate my gifts and abilities with the word "psychic". I do not foretell the future. I provide spiritual, intuitive guidance in the here and now for people's spiritual growth through life.

I was raised Catholic, then became a born-again Christian and deepened my personal relationship with Him and His word. I've spent my adult life practicing my faith in God/Jesus, learning how to hear Him through scripture and the various ways in which He has shown Himself to me in my life. This allows me to attest that the mastery of my intuition is a vehicle and a gift God uses to speak to me and through me. The work that I do is more than enough proof to me that it is indeed a ministry. God has used me as a vessel, as a channel to do His works, providing comfort and healing in peoples' lives from mental, emotional, physical, and spiritual healing. My prayer for the clients I work with is for God to channel through me whatever my client needs to know or heal in the present time for their spiritual journey.

Because at times, my work, my ministry, my passion, and my gifts, have been misunderstood and judged by my fellow Christians, I consider myself spiritual versus religious. I have found the former is more inclusive of everyone, which aligns with who I am as a person. I consider my intuition a blessing. Many religious people would argue and challenge my truth, but the beauty of it is, it is MY truth and my own personal relationship with God and how intimately I have come to know Him in my life. If you find yourself resonating with what you just read and perhaps have struggled with this yourself, know that you are not alone. I have many Christian friends and clients who are "spiritual". Follow your truth! If you are reading this book, it looks like you already are.

However, if quoting scripture is important to some reading this book to help reconcile their own discomfort with the topic, I would like to offer the following passage from Dr. Michael Bressem, who wrote an article called "Divination and the Bible" (2011). Dr. Bressem is my friend and mentor, and he holds a doctorate in Clinical Psychology from Western Seminary and also holds a master's degree in Theology.

Divination is the practice of finding out what the future may hold for you. Divinus is Latin means "godlike". It was therefore to have the omniscience, the foresight, of God concerning particular matters. The Bible takes two seemingly contradictory positions regarding divination: on one hand it forbids it, and on the other hand it was actively practiced by Hebrews and Christians alike in both old and new Testaments.

The main passage that people may say proves that divination is wrong is in Deuteronomy 18:10-12, 'There shall not be found among you anyone who...practices divination, or a soothsayer, or one who interprets omens, or a sorcerer, or one who conjures spells, or a medium...or one who calls up the dead. For all who do these things are an abomination to the Lord our God...' (see also Leviticus 19:26). Yet in a following verse it says, 'The Lord your God will raise up for you a Prophet like me [Moses] from among your own brothers (v15). Prophecy has a long history throughout Scripture: from the interpretation of Pharaoh's dreams by the patriarch Joseph (Genesis 41) to the visions of the Apostle John (Book of Revelation). A prophet's job was to speak for God usually about future matters. In other words, the prophet practiced divination. Prophesying is considered a spiritual gift (Romans 12:6) 1 Corinthians 13:2; 14:1 within the Bible.

Dr. Bressem's article goes into further detail and cites bible stories related to lot casting, signs and omens, interpreting dreams, receiving visions, and seeking signs, all of which were practiced. He concludes with: *"If the purpose is Godly, then likely almost any divinatory tool is okay."* I will cover more on this topic in various chapters as it pertains.

Lastly, people's uncertainty prevents them from unlocking their intuition. That is, they simply aren't sure how to use it. They believe in intuition and want to learn how to develop it and even master it. This population has perhaps even experienced their spiritual awakening already, which in essence, is the rite of passage to use your intuition as the gift it was intended to be. Whichever you identify with: those who doubt, those who fear, or those who are uncertain, you have come to the right place. You are not here by accident. This is your appointed date and time, and I am honored to walk this life-changing journey with you.

Notes

The Imposter

Now that we know what intuition is, let's learn what it is not. A key part of developing your intuition is recognizing the "imposter" versus the "intuitive". In our lives, we may encounter many imposters but none more important than the one that resides within. We must spend time unpacking this in this chapter in order to store our baggage away—pun intended! So, who is this imposter? This imposter is none other than our subconscious mind.

Our subconscious mind is the master operating system in our brain and serves two important functions:

1) It is in charge of our "automatic" bodily functions, such as our breathing, digestion, heartbeat, and all our glandular secretions—basically, our autonomic nervous system. It regulates all these functions to include our fight-or-flight response, which provides our body with a burst of energy in order to respond to perceived dangers as well as

shuts down other unnecessary bodily functions to enable available resources to save our life when in danger. For example, if you're being attacked by a tiger, you don't need to be digesting your food. That energy or resource can be redirected to fleeing or fighting off the tiger. Can you imagine having to remind your organs to function every day or remind your body to fill you with adrenaline when in danger? I can barely keep track of all the reminders I have set on my phone, my calendar and all my sticky notes everywhere. If I had to remind my body to function, I wouldn't be writing this book right now. So, we can thank our subconscious for operating on autopilot. Well, at least when it comes to keeping us alive, anyway.

2) The second feature of our subconscious mind is that it is a data bank, a repository for information, a storage-house that houses all of our long-term memories. This includes our experiences, childhood, traumas, beliefs, feelings, emotions, habits of thinking, acting and behaving. Not all things stored are necessarily good for us or serve us well as adults, yet these things are also on autopilot and completely outside of our conscious awareness. Let me preface that there are two forms of trauma, big T and little T, as they refer to them in psychology. It's important to understand this because we have ALL experienced trauma, and until we fully bring it into our conscious awareness to process and integrate, it will manifest itself in our adult life through our perceptions, beliefs, reactions, and behaviors. Otherwise known as "The Imposter".

"Big T" traumas are the ones we readily associate as trauma because they are often significant, deeply disturbing events that leave a person feeling hopeless or powerless, often incapable of integrating the situation or circumstances into their current reality. Examples would be those who have been exposed to war, combat, natural disasters, physical or sexual abuse, terrorism, or catastrophic accidents. These are some of the most profound and debilitating experiences one can endure. However, a person does not have to undergo an overtly distressing event for it to affect them. An accumulation of smaller or less pronounced events can still be traumatic but in the small 't' form. These are distressing events that can be beyond a person's ability to cope and leave them feeling hopeless, but they do not necessarily cause life-threatening or bodily-threatening outcomes (i.e. divorce, infidelity, having a child, bullying, interpersonal conflict, financial difficulty).

The most difficult aspect of dealing with these sorts of "little t" traumas is that there can be a tendency to overlook them because of the thought or belief that: 1) Many people experience them. It's just a part of life. 2) One small 't' shouldn't cause that much long-term distress.

> While one small 't' trauma may not lead to significant distress, multiple compounded small 't' traumas, particularly in a short span of time, are more likely to lead to an increase in distress and trouble with emotional functioning. These traumas may have occurred over the course of one's life or condensed in the recent past. Also, everyone experiences trauma differently and largely dependent on a person's predisposing factors, as well as if there was significant avoidance in their ability to process their experience. Any event can be deemed traumatic to the degree that it undermines a person's sense of safety in the world, physical or emotional. (Barbash, 2017, para 7)

So, both forms of trauma, along with our other long-term memories, childhood, and past experiences (mostly the bad ones) have formed our beliefs. All of this now lives in your subconscious mind, along with any thoughts, feelings, emotional reactions, habits and behaviors you have surrounding them. Remember how your subconscious helps your heartbeat automatically go into fight-or-flight to keep you alive from the tiger? It does the same thing in this area of your life as well. It's on automatic response mode and reacts by fighting or fleeing too (defense-mode) when those painful memories are triggered. Same system, same response, all **below** our conscious awareness (**sub**conscious) or too far down and repressed (**un**conscious).

The subconscious mind is completely impersonal and automatic in its functions. It is a 'reaction machine' which tries to give you ... 'directions' in terms of emotions ... [It] files, in your memory (data storage unit), everything that happens to you, whether good or bad. Based on the conscious mind's interpretation of these experiences, the subconscious develops automatic or pre-programmed courses of behavior which are called habits or habit patterns. It can neither judge, evaluate or discriminate. Further, if the information sent to the subconscious by the conscious mind is distorted or inaccurate, then the "robot" subconscious will file in your memory distorted or inaccurate data. In summary, your subconscious mind is strictly an impersonal intake mechanism which dutifully accepts all communications sent to it by your conscious mind, whether it is right, wrong or distorted. It freely provides (via a "scanning mechanism") the conscious mind with all kinds of memory data, though particularly distasteful experiences of the past are repressed and beyond conscious recall. The "scanning mechanism" of your brain is truly a fantastic one; it can look over all the available information in the subconscious mind in an instant. The available information in the human brain is contained in some 10 billion memory cells, each capable of storing 100,000 bits of information. (Atman, 2020)

According to cognitive neuroscientists, we are only conscious of 5% of our cognitive activity, so most of our decisions, actions, emotions and behavior depends on 95% of our brain activity that goes beyond our conscious awareness. (Fannin and Williams, n.d.)

WOW! Read that again. It is estimated that we only have 5% conscious awareness and a whopping 95% is subconscious. You may find some other data that estimates 10/90, but nonetheless, it is truly mind-blowing. Sorry, the puns just keep unintentionally coming.

Psychologist Sigmund Freud used the iceberg metaphor to illustrate this: (*Note that the term subconscious and unconscious will be used interchangeably throughout this book)

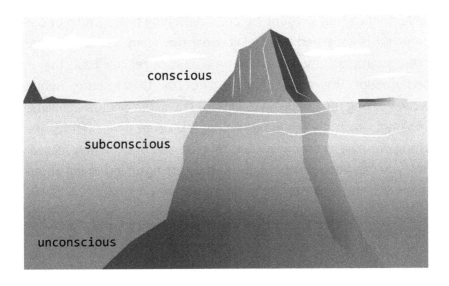

The tip above the water that is visible is the conscious mind, the 5%. This is your thinking/analyzing mind, your current awareness at any given time, your perceptual reality. It has short-term memory with limited capacity. Like an iceberg, there's so much more than meets the eye. So much more underneath the water that is hidden, which we don't see nor readily have access to. Herein lives your subconscious mind: this vast storage house and memory bank, which houses all your past memories and is virtually unlimited in storage capacity. Every day as we are going about our lives, observing, and interacting with the world around us, we have a filtered and skewed lens that we wear. Everything we do, see, hear, say or feel is automatically filtered through this lens. It takes that information, in our present moment, and screens it against the beliefs that live in our subconscious mind. It will analyze it and then either accept or reject it based on the previously stored information. A system of checks and balances, and it does all that in a split second, with a blink of its lens.

As you can imagine, just like the movie "The Titanic", that 95% hidden underneath the ocean can wreak havoc in our lives, and we have no idea that's where we are functioning from. Much of our behavior is governed by our subconscious mind. Consider these other examples of what we do on a daily or regular basis that is on autopilot. They are neither good nor bad, they just are: driving a car, walking up and down a flight of stairs, our posture, smiling, blinking, our body language, riding a bike, or other habits like biting our nails or bouncing our knee up and down when seated. Yes, you can become conscious of these things if you think about them, but the majority of the time they are on autopilot without us giving them a second thought because they have just become second nature.

Remember when we first learned how to drive a car? We had to study the manual and learn all the rules of the road: what each sign meant, what each line on the road meant, how far we had to start braking to come to a stop before a traffic light, how to properly do a lane change, and what to do if there's a bus in front of us with flashing lights. Besides all that, we had to do certain things inside the car, like make sure we wore our seat belts, adjust the seat, adjust the side and rearview mirrors, make sure we had gas, make sure we had our foot on the brake before putting the gear in reverse, etc. When we first started driving, it was a whole production. We felt nervous. It was more methodical. We were consciously aware of what we were doing. Our eyes were vigilantly on the lookout for anything around us.

Fast forward to today, when you get into your car, you do those things automatically. When you are driving, your mind is no longer overly focused. It feels safe to wander elsewhere, like pondering what you need to do when you get to work, whether you want to stop at Starbucks en route or not, making a phone call to a friend, reflecting on a conversation you had last week, singing along to a song on the radio, getting excited and salivating thinking about what you want to have for lunch...for dinner...for dessert!! (Just me again? Ok. Geez, tough crowd!) Your mind is no longer in hypervigilant mode like it was when you were a novice. It wanders. In fact, for many people, driving is therapeutic. Their mind detaches and zones out. That's why when some people are upset, they'll go for a drive. It allows your conscious mind to disconnect. I've had some of my best ideas while driving. In fact, so many creative downloads would come to me that I had to start doing voice recordings on my phone instead of trying to jot it down with one hand on the wheel. This somewhat of a meditative state when we are driving is one of the reasons why people get pulled over by cops, not realizing they were going over the speed limit. By people, I mean me. Any other takers? Moving on...

Storytime

I had a 30-year-old female client, let's call her Kaitlyn, who came to see me regularly about her love life. Every three months, she would make an appointment to get guidance on her situation with her current boyfriend. She always found herself in the same predicament of "choosing the wrong guys". When one relationship would end, she was right back out there finding another one. It was this vicious cycle, every three to four months. She never wanted to be alone, so there was this endless revolving door of welcoming new male friends into her life. They would always start out as friends, then things would progress pretty quickly, and suddenly they're dating. She thinks he's the one. She's over the moon. She's gushing about how great he is, how he comes over every single day, he practically lives there, they spend every waking hour together, and she's in sooooo in love. All this by week two.

Fast-forward three months later, she's back in my office. Things have changed: he barely comes over, she sits by her phone waiting for a text or call, she's putting in way more than she's receiving, he's unreliable—he says he'll be over and then cancels at the last minute or doesn't even call at all. She would find herself always being the one to initiate time together as he would rather be out with his friends, drinking, having fun, while she's at home with a box of Kleenex. Rinse and repeat.

Kaitlyn and I had several spiritual counseling sessions together, intuitive readings, and we also did an inner-child healing journey, all of which pointed back to her childhood experiences, her trauma wounds. Kaitlyn grew up without the presence of her father. He was in and out of her life because he was an alcoholic. He made false promises and never delivered on any of them. She had many experiences in which he was supposed to come to pick her up to spend time with her and would never show up. No phone call, no nothing. He was absent all of her childhood and was constantly disappointing her. She would sometimes get her hopes up, especially around her birthday or holidays, only to be left disappointed time and time again.

Because of these painful experiences, at such a young age, Kaitlyn developed unconscious beliefs about herself, such as being unworthy of love, fear of abandonment, that there must be something wrong with her, that she's unlovable, that she has to work for the love and attention she so deeply desires, that she's not good enough, and that men will disappoint her and not be there for her. She has carried these unconscious beliefs since she was a child, and it's now playing out in her adulthood.

She would get too easily and quickly attached to her partners, constantly fearing that she would be abandoned and disappointed again. So, she would overcompensate for this by being too clingy and needy, having unrealistic expectations of her partners in terms of the time and energy they should be spending together. She had a hole in her heart so big that she kept trying to fill outside of herself when what she really needed to do was heal inside herself.

When Kaitlyn made this connection, it was both an "a-ha moment" for her and a very painful one. She had an oozing, bleeding wound that she never touched inside. The thing is, we repeat what we don't heal. It is not a surprise that Kaitlyn would attract similar life experiences that would sting that wound because, without it, she would never have the awareness of the true emotional impact of those earlier childhood experiences. When she realized this was truly a journey about herself, she could bring more conscious awareness around her choices, her actions, her patterns. It required a lot of work on Kaitlyn's part to shift her deeply rooted beliefs and to refrain from continuing to seek those trauma bonds with partners. It can almost feel like a drug to seek that hit, of going into that cycle because it is what is comfortable for her.

Kaitlyn had one or two more of those trauma bonds, then six months later, she had enough. She spent some time with herself and sat with the discomfort of being lonely. She did the work to unlearn her behaviors. She began to love herself, giving her own self what she had been so desperately seeking: time, attention, priority, love. There were lots of tears and pain throughout her process. This was not a quick, overnight fix. I didn't hear from her for a while, and one day, I received a text. Kaitlyn was in such a good place in her life. She was in a much healthier relationship that was interdependent and not codependent. She had a stronger sense of self and felt so empowered, having embraced all aspects of herself and released what no longer served her. When she did that, she was able to attract the right type of person who could match the same frequency she was at. Because at the end of the day, relationships are brought into our lives to serve as a mirror to us.

Unveiling the imposter within us is necessary and empowering. It is the healing we are called to do, so we can strip away all that holds us back. Not identifying this aspect of ourselves and how it manifests in our lives can have life-changing and long-term consequences on our personal and professional life, and our relationships (with ourselves and with others). It can deceive us, skew our perceptions, and keep us from living our truth. It can cause and perpetuate our own self-inflicting suffering and unhappiness. We must be able to discern which part of ourselves is at the forefront at any given time in our lives. Who is making the decisions? Based on what frame of reference? Which lens are we perceiving things through? The work is within, and so is our intuition. In order to develop and learn to trust it, it needs to be at the forefront with a clear view ahead.

Notes

The Comp"YOU"ter

Now let's talk about the word: "PROGRAMMING". What are some thoughts or things you affiliate with that word? Perhaps a computer as in "computer programming", or other electronics you program, like your alarm to wake you up each morning, or your DVR to record your favorite show, or your coffee maker to automatically brew in the morning?

Whichever electronic device you program, whether it's a DVR, coffee maker, computer or cell phone, the purpose and goal is to automate it to produce a desired and expected result by entering in specific data instructing it to do so. Even if you entered something in error (like the wrong time or channel) it doesn't know that, does it? It simply accepts it and produces what was entered. It simply acts on the programming. This is a metaphor for what has happened in our subconscious mind as well.

During our early childhood years, from birth to about six to seven years of age, our brain is functioning primarily in Alpha and Theta brainwave cycles. This means our brain is basically in a constant meditative, twilight state. We are in a super learning state, open to suggestion and completely impressionable, absorbing everything around us like a sponge. This is the stage where memory happens. Babies are learning to play peek-a-boo with you, you can teach them objects using flashcards, teach them how to say "Mama" or "Dada" or "Nana". They mirror everything you show them.

Brainwaves

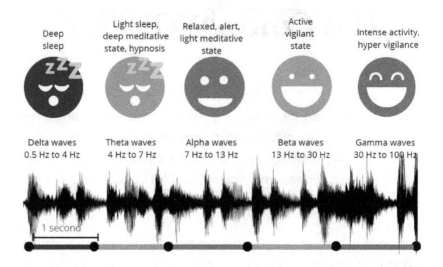

Deep sleep	Light sleep, deep meditative state, hypnosis	Relaxed, alert, light meditative state	Active vigilant state	Intense activity, hyper vigilance
Delta waves 0.5 Hz to 4 Hz	Theta waves 4 Hz to 7 Hz	Alpha waves 7 Hz to 13 Hz	Beta waves 13 Hz to 30 Hz	Gamma waves 30 Hz to 100 Hz

1 second

As a point of reference, let's understand the different brainwaves we experience in our adult lives today:

*There are four categories of these brainwaves, ranging from the most activity to the least activity. When the brain is aroused and actively engaged in mental activities, it generates **beta** waves...which are the fastest of the four different brainwaves...Beta waves are characteristics of a strongly engaged mind. A person in active conversation* *would be in beta. A debater would be in high beta. A person making a speech, or a teacher, or a talk show host would all be in beta when they are engaged in their work.*

*The next brainwave category in order of frequency is **alpha**. Where beta represented arousal, alpha represents non-arousal. Alpha brainwaves are slower...A person who has completed a task and sits down to rest is often in an alpha state. A person who takes time out to reflect or meditate is usually in an alpha state. A person who takes a break from a conference and walks in the garden is often in an alpha state.*

*The next state, **theta** brainwaves, are (of even) slower frequency...A person who has taken time off from a task and begins to daydream is often in a theta brainwave state. A person who is driving on a freeway and discovers that they can't recall the last five miles, is often in a theta state - induced by the process of freeway driving. The repetitious nature of that form of driving compared to a country road would differentiate a theta state and a beta state in order to perform the driving task safely.*

Individuals who do a lot of freeway driving often get good ideas, as they are in theta. Individuals who run outdoors often are in the state of mental relaxation that is slower than alpha and when in theta, they are prone to a flow of ideas. This can also occur in the shower or tub or even while shaving or brushing your hair. It is a state where tasks become so automatic that you can mentally disengage from them.

*The final brainwave state is **delta**. Here the brainwaves are of (the) slowest frequency...They never go down to zero* *because that would mean that you were brain dead. But, deep dreamless sleep would take you down to the lowest frequency.*

When we go to bed and read for a few minutes before attempting sleep, we are likely to be in low beta. When we put the book down, turn off the lights and close our eyes, our brainwaves will descend from beta, to alpha, to theta and finally, when we fall asleep, to delta. ("What is the function of the various brainwaves?" 1997)

Hey, wake up! No falling asleep reading THIS book. I need you back in low beta, chop-chop! Fascinating stuff though, right?

So, going back to our early childhood, we now understand how our mind accepts every piece of information as true because there are not yet any existing belief systems based on previous experiences that could contradict the new information. This is how we develop firm beliefs in early childhood that impact us for the rest of our lives, both positively and negatively. They are permanently downloaded and put into the blueprint of our mind which becomes increasingly difficult to change. If you were around grandma a lot growing up, you received a lot of programming from her beliefs. If you were around your mom's boyfriend who wasn't kind to you and modeled bad or unhealthy behaviors, you were programmed based on that experience and how that made you feel, whether you felt safe or not. If you were raised by an anxious or depressed parent and you were around a lot of stress, negative self-talk, anger, etc. that is in your programming too.

From that time on, when new information is presented (age seven through adulthood), your subconscious mind evaluates it against its existing beliefs and will accept or reject it accordingly, as we previously discussed. Yet, all those programmed beliefs were placed there and suggested by somebody else. You were never given a choice. This now becomes the foundation for our perception of the world around us. These beliefs we hold about ourselves and life remain in our subconscious throughout the rest of our lives. But they will show up in our behaviors, reactions (triggers), esteem, relationships, achievements, goals, or lack thereof, how we choose our friends, our life partners and so on. It's now easy to see how our early childhood experiences are such a key factor in determining the adult we become. St. Francis Xavier, who was a Spanish Basque religious leader, saint, and apostle to India in the 1500s, must have been onto something, even way back then, when he said, *"Give me a child for the first seven years, and I'll give you the man."* It is who we become. It is who we are...or is it really?

Now stay with me here and let's take this just one step further with a visualization and continue the metaphor to truly understand how this all works together and shows up in our everyday adult life. I want you to think of yourself as the computer (subconscious mind). Inside you is software that is programmed (in the form of adopted beliefs, experiences, memories). Every computer needs an anti-virus system. Its job is to screen and filter everything that is being received by your computer and scan it for anything that looks suspicious or may be a threat. Its job is to flag and warn you of any imminent danger, avoid infiltration, and keep your computer safe. This anti-virus protection is called your ego.

We've all heard the term ego before, perhaps in laymen's terms. You might hear someone saying: "Ugh, Bob's got such a huge ego. He's always bragging about his career success, how much money he makes, the expensive car he drives, his designer clothes, all the

beautiful women he has as arm candy, etc. He's so full of himself."
So, in this context, we are referring to Bob being overly confident,
the way he presents himself and how he wants to be perceived by
others, being a "show-off", and gauging his self-worth on material
things. Yes, the ego is about "me, me, me, look at me," but this
example is the most basic, superficial understanding of our ego.

People tend to have a limited understanding of the ego, and
without fully understanding all the intricacies that make up the
ego, you will always be a slave to this part of "self". Ego in Latin
literally means, "I or the self." However, this is not our real self. This
identity is based on our subconscious mind, which we now realize
is an identity we formed from birth to seven years old: *"The ego
is a mental construct of who we believe we are based on our past
experience" (LePera, 2020).*

Our ego is actually very complex and dynamic, but its primary
function is to preserve our (false) identity. AT ALL COSTS! It is the
voice of our subconscious mind.

Until we understand that our ego has been at the forefront of our
lives, perceiving and reacting to the world based on false or limiting
beliefs, we will be a slave to that super-reactive place inside us
that is activated by someone else's behaviors or comments. *"The
ego creates a story. It assigns meaning to our experiences based
on our past experiences. Sometimes these narratives can be very
painful and keep us repeating familiar patterns. Keeping us out of
alignment with who we truly are" (LePera, 2021).*

Here are some examples of common triggers for our fragile ego:

Someone rejecting you.
Someone leaving you (or the threat that they will).
Someone discounting or ignoring you.
Someone being unavailable to you.
Someone giving you a disapproving look.
Someone blaming or shaming you.
Someone being judgmental or critical of you.
Someone being too busy to make time for you.
Someone not appearing to be happy to see you.
Someone trying to control you.
Someone betraying you.
Someone being needy or trying to smother you.
Someone treating you unjustly or someone else you love unjustly.
Someone challenging your beliefs.
Someone excluding you.

Here are some of our egoic reactions when we experience triggers:

I get angry. I lash out.
I get needy.
I comply. I become a people-pleaser.
I shut down and withdraw from the other person.
I blame someone else for my pain.
I turn to an addiction—food, drugs, alcohol, sex, porn, shopping, work, gambling, and so on.
I throw a tantrum.
I run.

> *I avoid.*
> *I deny.*
> *I hurt.*
> *(Paul, 2020)*

When triggered, we tend to respond in an aggressive way that we will likely regret later. Our reaction is so heightened and intense because we're defending a painful feeling that has surfaced.

> *Each person is so identified with the thoughts that make up their opinion, that those thoughts harden into mental positions which are invested with a sense of self. In other words: Identity and thought merge. Once this has happened, when I defend my opinions (thoughts), I feel and act as if I were defending my very self. Unconsciously, I feel and act as if I were fighting for survival and so my emotions will reflect this unconscious belief. They become turbulent. I am upset, angry, defensive, or aggressive. I need to win at all costs lest I become annihilated. That's the illusion. The ego doesn't know that mind and mental positions have nothing to do with who you are because the ego is the unobserved mind itself. (Tolle, 2008)*

This can truly wreak havoc and all hell can break loose. It can leave us feeling re-traumatized and exhausted in the aftermath. We may also try to correct other people because we think they are wrong or feel like people are difficult and irritating. We may feel like we're putting up with people's B.S. and having to bite our tongues instead of going off on someone we think is deserving of our wrath. One of the patterns of the ego is to be right and make everyone else wrong. The ego turns things around and makes it about the other person. This is one of the main forms of unconsciousness.

The truth of the matter is, we are ALL functioning off our ego/ subconscious self until we do the inner work. *"The ego isn't wrong; it's just unconscious. When you observe the ego in yourself, you are beginning to go beyond it. Don't take the ego too seriously. When you detect ego behavior in yourself, smile. At times you may even laugh"* (Tolle, 2008).

Consider who and what triggers you, upsets you, irritates you, hurts you, pisses you off, offends you, takes you to the point of no return, and gets a rise out of you in any way. It is likely they are serving as your mirror to what you need to heal because if it were not so, you wouldn't have had such a strong reaction in the first place. Remember, it's not about who or what is right or wrong. It's about holding space for all opinions as they are not personal to you, even though it may feel like it. When we choose to let go of identifying ourselves with our mind, our true, authentic self emerges.

Let's take a look at what our ego may look like in our everyday lives:

Scenario 1: You've slaved over a hot stove to cook a delicious dinner for your spouse, but he comes home late without calling.

Ego felt: "He is rude and inconsiderate for not even calling. I do so much for him, and this is what I get?"

Awareness of truth: As I sit here alone at the table, I feel unappreciated, disrespected, and invisible, just like my mom made me feel as a child.

Scenario 2: You texted your new boyfriend this morning to say I love you, and he didn't text back all day.

Ego felt: "What did I do to upset him? Is he cheating on me? Does he still love me?"

Awareness of truth: When I didn't get a timely response, I felt feelings of fear, insecurity and mistrust. I wasn't modeled a healthy relationship growing up. Dad cheated on Mom and left us. She wrote off all men as liars and cheaters. I felt Dad must not love me to leave me like that.

Scenario 3: You've been working on an important project at work and the day has come to finally show it to your boss. You are so excited about all the work you put into it. You couldn't wait to see his reaction, but when you showed it to him, he didn't seem very excited. In fact, he made some changes to it.

Ego felt: Deflated, let down, rejected, failure. "Nothing I ever do is ever good enough. I can never please my boss."

Awareness of truth: When I was small, my dad never told me or showed me he was proud of me. He corrected everything I did. He would embarrass me in little league by always telling me what I was doing wrong in front of my friends. I was never good enough.

Let's take this awareness a step further and consider all the other possible explanations in scenario #2 of why she didn't receive a reply to his text:

1) Maybe he got busy in his day and overlooked the text or thought he replied

2) Maybe his phone ran out of battery

3) Maybe the text never reached him due to connectivity issues

4) Maybe he replied, and his text never reached her

5) Maybe not every text needs a reply and people can just appreciate the message and feel secure and confident in the relationship

There are countless reasons, yet her mind goes straight to her subconscious wounding and takes it personally. To bring the subconscious to the conscious is to recognize these types of scenarios and observe how they are playing out in the current time. We must learn to retrain and reframe the mind from our trauma thoughts, despite how our emotions and nervous system may feel because it will feel "real" to us in that space (perceived danger). But the truth is, there is no real danger there. Just a perceived danger from a painful childhood experience and memory that we now have an opportunity to heal.

The rule of thumb, if you take away anything from this segment is:

- **Pause. Observe your reaction.**
- **Seek to understand versus assume or expect.**
- **Respond versus react.**
- **Use "I" statements.**

Using "I" statements is a style of communication recommended by psychologists because it focuses on your feelings rather than your thoughts or characteristics about the other person. Once we recognize our wounds, we can sit with this and realize it's not about the other person, but it's still okay for us to make requests with our preferences. Keeping with scenario #2, you can simply state your desires and requests if something bothers you or you'd like something different. You can always use this phrasing:

"When I or when you _____, I feel/felt _____. I would love it/appreciate it if (make your request) _____ that would help me feel _____. Would you be willing to do that for me?"

So, using the above phrasing, here's an example of what you can say:

"When I <u>didn't get a reply to my text</u>, I felt <u>bothered about it all day</u>. I would love it if <u>you could acknowledge and reply to my text next time</u> because <u>that would help me feel secure and loved</u>. Would you be willing to do that for me?"

That may feel very vulnerable to say, but it is the truth. Often, we mask the truth because of our pride or ego. We may use other words that don't make us feel as vulnerable, and then we wonder why people don't understand us. Believe it or not, the majority of the time, we are speaking very indirectly, trying to use "fluff words" or "hints" hoping the other person can read our mind. Or we will say something vague to "soften" what we are saying.

With the example above, your tone in saying it is equally, if not more, important than what you're actually saying. We want to speak in a loving, calm, neutral place of no blame. This is the tricky part because if you feel like you are saying this just "to be nice" and "deal with" the other person's wrongdoing, then that in and of itself is still ego. We must be humbled and truly understand this is about our "preferences" and we can't demand it, but we can request it. Remove the right/wrong aspect. This may be a hard concept to understand, agree with and implement, but I am offering it to you to ponder in your inner work. I know from first-hand experience that it will make life so much more beautiful when we own our piece and express it from a place of request, not demands, and without assumptions, expectations, judgement, or blame. In other words, without ego!

Even though this phrasing seems like a lot of work at first, it should actually be part of our everyday language instead of demanding things of others as if we are entitled in some way. Unfortunately, we didn't come into this world with a communication manual, so undoing what comes naturally to all of us is going to feel foreign. We must also realize that other people may not respond in the same way we communicated (with love, neutrality, kindness) because they are functioning from ego too, with a veil over their eyes. No matter how kindly we say it, such as using "I" versus "you", the other person could still blame us and say we're too sensitive and outright refuse to grant whatever our request was. Their language may be coming from a place of defense too. It is less likely this will happen when we use the right words and tone and most of all, our intention is in the right place. At the end of the day, we can only control our own words, our own actions, and reactions, not others. We must continue to do better for ourselves and realize we are all growing, stretching, and evolving in our own way and in our own time. This is about peace for yourself regardless of what others do or don't do. Amen?!

If you didn't have an ideal childhood, all is not lost. Even if you had a seemingly wonderful childhood, I would caution that there are still many, many experiences and beliefs that you hold true today that could potentially (and likely) be negatively impacting your life and especially those who are closest to you and whom you love.

Food for thought: if when we were impressionable, programmable, and believed everything as truth while we were in a state of hypnosis (Alpha and Theta brainwaves), what would happen and could happen if we entered a state of hypnosis in our current adult age? What could we impress upon it now, today? Wow! (Insert mic drop here.) Things that make you go, "Hmmm," right? How do we break through that anti-virus software? Well, this is one of several ways. Have you ever tried hypnosis before? I have, several times, in fact. I am a huge fan! It actually helped me quit smoking after just one session. It's true!

Storytime

I had started dabbling with cigarettes at the age of about 12. (I know, I know. This is a judgement-free zone, remember?) I was the youngest of seven children, and pretty much all my siblings were smokers, with the exception of two. I was around it all the time growing up. Not only from my siblings, but from my uncles, aunts, and family friends. Remember, we're impressionable when we're younger. It seemed pretty glamorous and cool to be a smoker in the '70s when I was growing up. So, by high school, I was a smoker. I snuck cigarettes from my big brother since I was too young to buy them myself or I smoked with my grandmother—we all did, actually. She was so "cool" when it came to that. She claimed there was nothing wrong with it, and besides, she "never inhaled anyway" (as the smoke was funneling out through her nose). A vision of former President Clinton came to mind while I just typed that. (Not a reflection of my political views one way or the other, by the way.) Anyway, I digress...

The point being, I became a smoker and quit in 1997, one year before I became pregnant with my daughter Cassidy, who was born in 1999. That was intentional. I wanted my body to be in the best possible health. The process took a good four to eight weeks where my mind wasn't obsessed with the thoughts of smoking, or in this case, not smoking as well. I first started chewing Nicorette gum in the hopes that I wouldn't have withdrawals. I started with the lowest dose and even cut the gum in half, but I still had awful side effects. I started trembling, felt nauseous, and light-headed. I guess it was too much for someone who smoked ½ a pack to ¾ of a pack a day, or perhaps I was just sensitive and didn't know it then. So, I ditched that awful idea and decided I would just do it cold turkey.

I used to smoke menthols, so I thought if I replaced it with a sugar-free mint candy or gum, that would work fine. So, I did. It was hard at first because the cravings were miserable. I was super irritable, especially during certain times like when having my coffee first thing in the morning, or having a cocktail, or out with my friends hanging out, or driving in the car. If you're a smoker or former smoker, you can relate and maybe even have a reaction, like salivating, as you read that. So, I quit from 1997 to 2011, 14 long years. Wow, I was super proud of myself. First try and I succeeded! It definitely wasn't easy, especially during the first two to three weeks, but it got easier over time. Plus, I was motivated knowing I wanted to have a baby soon.

Fast forward to 2011, I was going through my divorce and started going clubbing with my girlfriends, drinking, dancing, just having some fun with the girls. A few of them were smokers, so I went from having an occasional cigarette they'd offer me, to eventually buying my own pack so as to not "bum one" off of them (that's smoker talk, FYI). Well, apparently, I can't be a part-time smoker. I'm either in or out! I quickly got addicted to the nicotine again after a few months and formed an expensive habit I really couldn't afford, now being a single mom. Plus, the cost of a pack of cigarettes sky-rocketed by then.

In hindsight, relapsing into becoming a smoker again back then was definitely an outlet for my stress during the divorce. I remember being at work (on the Marine Corps base) and no one ever knew me as a smoker in all the years I worked there. When they saw me out in the courtyard smoking for the first time, they were all shocked and had to do a double-take. "CIELO? IS THAT YOU?!?" I think they all secretly knew I must've been going through something pretty serious to do a 180 like that. I may have actually had a few Marines (co-workers and clients alike) directly ask me or others if I was ok. Such a rebel I was!

After two years of smoking again, I decided I wanted to quit and try the same cold-turkey technique I did back in 1997. After all, "It wasn't all that bad. I can do it. Piece of cake."

It's kind of like when a woman goes through childbirth and people say, "Oh, you'll forget all the pain once the baby is born." Uh newsflash, that pain is not forgettable. Needless to say, with everything I was going through at the time, and using smoking as a crutch for my stress, quitting didn't fare well this time around, so I thought I'd try something kinder to myself rather than ripping off the proverbial band-aid. With that, I booked an appointment with a hypnotherapist in Honolulu that came highly recommended.

Like most people who hear the word "hypnosis", I had some preconceived ideas about what it would be like. I mean, let's face it, most of us have only seen someone being hypnotized while watching some magic show where the magician calls up some unassuming person in the audience and puts them in a trance-like state to then embarrass them by suggesting some silly things for them to do or say, all to the audience's delight and entertainment. Hysterical laughing ensues, the person "wakes up" with a snap of the magician's finger, a bit disoriented and seemingly has no memory of the whole thing as the audience cheers and the person makes their way back to their seat, blushing, and their friend leans over to whisper something in their ear and the camera fades out...Does that sound about accurate?

Well, hypnotherapists, or Neuro-Linguistic Programming Practitioners (NLP), know this reputation they have all too well. So, before they even work with you, they spend some time debunking all the myths about hypnosis and really explain the truth of how it all works. Simply said: "Learning NLP is like learning the language of your own mind!"

"Neuro" (for Neurology) – The physical components as well as the mental and emotional components of our neurology

"Linguistic" – Pertains to the language that you use, and more specifically, how you communicate with others and more importantly, how you communicate with yourself

"Programming" – (Function) Perceiving your mind as your internal operating system, programming is the way our past experiences, thoughts and emotions affect all areas of our lives. (nlp.com, 2021)

The basis of hypnosis lies in reprogramming or retraining our subconscious mind. You can choose whatever issue you want to work on: confidence, success, weight-loss, sports performance, self-esteem, stress relief, finances, sales, or ending any bad habit to name a few.

This insight (of the ability to reprogram our mind) is profound because it reveals that we are not creating the lives we desire but are unconsciously (through the subconscious mind) manifesting lives that are coherent with the beliefs we downloaded as children. Since up to 70% of the downloaded beliefs acquired before age 7 are disempowering, self-sabotaging, or limiting, we experience stress from the programs that undermine our conscious mind's wishes, desires and aspirations. (Lipton, 2019, para 6)

Indeed because, *"We do not see things as they are. We see things as we are" (Nachmani).* Hypnosis is a powerful tool I can personally attest to. I had one session for my smoking cessation and never had to go back. Why? Because smoking is a habit, and habits reside in our subconscious mind and therefore on autopilot. Mindy Ash, Clinical Hypnotherapist, who had a practice in Honolulu and has since moved to Las Vegas, was my hypnotherapist back then. She also tackled my "beliefs" about smoking and quitting smoking in our sessions. Most of our programmed beliefs are fear-based, by the way. The fears she reprogrammed were around the following thoughts: It's hard to quit. I will gain weight. My social life won't be as fun or satisfying. I can't do it this time around. I need to smoke to destress myself and cope.

Until I met Mindy and tried hypnosis, I probably had the same impressions about it that you do. The truth is, when undergoing a hypnosis session with a professional practitioner, you are actually very much aware and remain in control of your actions at every moment. In fact, you have the power to terminate your session at any time, although there would really be no reason to. It is actually extremely relaxing. It feels like when you are about to fall asleep at night and feel very relaxed or when you are just barely waking up in the morning. In that space, your mind can be impressed upon to receive new beliefs, those that serve you better to achieve your own personal goals. Thoughts and beliefs that YOU choose to implant there. This may need to be done repetitively to reprogram deep-rooted beliefs because, like driving a car or riding a bike, it gets better with repetition. You can also choose to try self-hypnosis via guided meditation as well. There are even programs and apps that use binaural beats for meditation that match the frequency and hertz of our brainwaves. I personally prefer to work with someone one-on-one as it is more customizable.

If hypnosis is not your forte to reprogram your subconscious mind of its beliefs and triggers, Dr. Judith Orloff offers some other things you can try:

Use these strategies to start healing your emotional triggers.

Be aware. In your journal, identify your top three emotional triggers which cause you to be most upset and thrown off balance. For instance, when someone criticizes your weight or appearance? Or if you don't earn a certain income? Or perhaps you feel unlovable and undeserving of a healthy relationship? Write these down to clarify the aspects of yourself that need to heal.

Track the trigger's origin. Journal about where these triggers originated. For example, did your parents say that you were "too fat" or unattractive? Did a teacher tell you that you didn't have what it takes to succeed in school? Or were you neglected by your family, so you grew up feeling unlovable? Knowing where your triggers come from allows you to know yourself better.

Reprogram negative beliefs. Start with one trigger that has the least emotional charge and begin to compassionately reprogram it. Tell yourself, "This is not reality." What's actually true is, "I am lovable, capable and smart." Substitute the negative belief with a positive, more realistic one.

Act as if. At the start of the healing process, you might need to "act as if" when you haven't fully integrated a new positive belief. That's okay. For instance, simply saying to someone, "I disagree. I fully deserve this great job" (even when you don't fully believe that) paves the way for a deeper belief later on. Sometimes you need to practice a more enlightened behavior for it to sink in and become real.

Work with a therapist or coach. It's often useful to seek guidance to help you find the root of the trigger and process the feelings involved. You may feel tremendous rage or sadness that your family never believed in you, so you never learned to believe in yourself. Expressing and releasing the feelings allows you to heal the trigger and move on to embrace your true power.

Healing your triggers is liberating because you won't be thrown off or drained by people's inappropriate comments. They may still be annoying, but they won't have the power to zap you. The more you heal your emotional triggers, the more emotionally free you will be. (Orloff, 2018)

In summary, although our subconscious can be likened to a computer (comp**YOU**ter) that runs on programming, we can also update our software to prevent glitches or minimize malfunctions. We can continually upgrade and remove apps we no longer need or use that are weighing down our storage space. We can improve its overall functionality. Like a computer, we sometimes can't fully understand why our subconscious acts the way it does. It seems to have a mind of its own, it's stubborn and may need IT support. That support can come in the form of therapy through a psychologist, NLP, or spiritual healer. I could write a whole book just on this chapter, and I may have delved deeper than I had planned, but I do feel it is necessary to fully grasp the concept of our false self and all its various manifestations. I hope this chapter has done some of that. We are all a work-in-progress. I invite you to always be curious about why you feel a certain way as you go through life. Remove the other person out of the equation because it's easy to find fault in other people. But this journey is not about other people. It's about our self. Our true self. Our ego will always step in to protect us from pain or perceived pain and keep us living in our past, stuck in patterns and programming. But, we must continue to unveil the imposter (subconscious), the comp**YOU**ter (your programming), and its anti-virus protection system (ego).

Notes

Notes

4

Mind Your Own Busyness

"For intuition to develop, it requires a broad and empty mental field of energy." — Niranjan Seshadri

Have you taken inventory lately of how busy your mind is on any given day? We are a society of multi-taskers and somehow that has become something to be admired, respected and even sought-after in our jobs, our role as a parent, and as a student. We have bought into the belief that multi-tasking equals proficiency and somehow makes you dynamic. Well, like every belief we have formed, let's unpack and question this.

With the world at our fingertips and notifications coming straight into our phone when we receive a new email, text, or notification from Facebook, Instagram, LinkedIn, TikTok or Clubhouse, we are constantly bombarded. Have you ever been in the middle of something (a project, typing out an email, doing mom/dad things, out grocery shopping, eating, doing your homework, whatever it is) and stopped doing it to check your phone or email because of that little ding notification? Then, one reply becomes a non-stop thread of chatting, memes, and a stream of back and forths, whether it's text replies, message replies, likes, or emojis on our social media. What should have been a quick reply turns into hours, wasting your valuable time, energy and brain cells. It's like a vortex! This is what is referred to as noise. Noise is anything that takes you away from the present moment—a distraction.

Remember the days when you, and people in general, weren't so easily accessible? If you weren't home, people had to leave a message on your answering machine and you wouldn't get it till you got home. You could then choose to get back to them at a convenient time for you. There was no expectation (perceived or otherwise) that you had to do it within 5, 10, 30 minutes or an hour like there is now with a text or message. We are simply too busy nowadays, too accessible. Yes, our mind is designed to be in a beta state in waking hours, active and engaged. But as it stands now, the majority of our time is likely spent alternating between beta (active) and delta (asleep) state. We now know from chapter three that the sweet spot is in quieting and slowing our mind down to an alpha and theta state.

So, how do we slow down? Do we even know how to anymore? Do you fidget whenever you've tried yoga or guided meditation? Going through your never-ending "to-do list" in your head instead of "inhale and exhale" or citing that mantra that's supposed to make all your thoughts go away? Does reading the word "meditation" bring up preconceived ideas about what that practice is supposed to be? Does it make you think: "I tried that, and it didn't work or that would never work for me, my mind doesn't stop or that's only for

Buddhist monks." Newsflash: You are **supposed** to have thoughts because you are alive! Read that again. Even during meditation, you are supposed to have thoughts because you have a pulse, and your mind is simply doing its job. The mind thinks involuntarily like the heart beats involuntarily. This is perhaps the biggest misconception about meditation, that we're not "supposed to have thoughts", aka brain chatter. Thoughts **will** come up. Commanding them to go away and feeling like you've failed at meditation because they didn't is like commanding your heart to stop beating and feeling like you've failed yourself because it didn't (Emily Fletcher, 2020). Is that a crazy concept or what? The goal is to allow your thoughts to come up, acknowledge them, and not get attached to them. What do I mean by attachment? Here's an example:

You begin your meditation in a comfortable seated position and start with rhythmic breathing: two second inhales through the nose, four second exhales out through your mouth (chest and stomach rising with each inhale and chest and stomach lowering back with each exhale). Do this about three times. You then allow yourself to go into a normal breathing pattern (in and out through the nose) focusing on the breath. Then suddenly, you're thinking about what you want to have for dinner. You begin to ponder what choices you have: "Chinese, Japanese, Italian, fast-food, but oh wait...I just had Italian the other night and oh my gosh, that eggplant parmesan was to die for!" You begin craving a burger, then tell yourself you shouldn't because you'll have to work out an extra hour just to burn it off. So, you start contemplating your workout routine. Or think, "What workout routine? Ughhh I've been slacking off lately, maybe I should start running again...no, never mind, not in the dead of winter. Oh man, I better finish my Christmas shopping." As you think about what's on your list...wait, you still have to make the list. "Oh my gosh, what am I doing trying to meditate? I have so much to freaking do!! There aren't enough hours in the day." Do you see what I mean by attachment? You had a thought, and you went with it, hook, line and sinker! That's what our mind does—well, let me back up: our untrained mind. Our ego-self.

Ego forces "thinking" on the mind when the mind wants to be still. It constantly tries to take you out of the present moment using chatterbox thoughts and internal noise to stop you from connecting to your real self (the small still voice within). It's like that irritating fly that keeps flying around your face! Ego communicates to you through your self-talk of: "I need to be doing this!", "I should be doing that!" persuading you to believe that you need to be "doing" or accomplishing something because the ego gauges its worthiness on accomplishment. Ultimately, its biggest fear is your "unworthiness", so by doing things, you must then be worthy, right? That's the gauge of our worth—in the flesh, anyway.

So, now that we know what attachment looks like, let's explore detachment using the same exact scenario from earlier:

You begin your meditation in a comfortable seated position and start with rhythmic breathing: two second inhales through the nose, four second exhales out through your mouth (chest and stomach rising with each inhale and chest and stomach lowering back with each exhale). You allow yourself to go into a normal breathing pattern (in and out through the nose) focusing on the breath. Then suddenly, you're thinking about what you want to have for dinner. You acknowledge the thought, without any judgement or criticism, and gently allow it to float on by, and each thought thereafter, without getting pulled into it. You become a mere observer of your thoughts because your thoughts are separate from you. Even if you do get pulled into them, you still always have the choice to detach from them at any given time. That's the beauty of it. You have control over your thoughts; they do not have control over you. Here are a few detachment techniques that I've recommended to my clients from my own personal toolbox:

Using visual imagery, imagine any of the following:

- A box on top of your head, gently placing those thoughts in there
- A cloud floating by that you place your thoughts on and allow them to float on by
- A bright white light from the Heavens shining on the crown of your head and your thoughts going towards the light, effortlessly
- Your thoughts disintegrating as they form
- A big, blank movie theatre screen in front of you that you can project your thoughts onto as they disappear into darkness

While doing this, you simultaneously keep focusing on your breath. Feeling the cool air enter in and out through your nostrils, allowing it to nourish your mind and body. The breath is always your anchor and what you keep going back to if your mind continues to wander.

Now, as with all things, practice makes progress. Meditation is about training the mind, just like you would train your biceps at the gym. The more you do those curls, the more blood flow to your biceps, the stronger they get. Same with the mind. If you do not currently have a meditative practice, I personally recommend you try doing it this way first: for the first week, do it on a daily basis (anytime, anywhere). You could be at work behind your desk, at home laying down to take a nap or at night before going to bed. It could be the first thing you do when you wake up, or at any place or time of your choosing (just don't do this while driving, in the shower or standing up). Set an alarm for five minutes, that's it. Try five minutes a day, with your eyes closed, nothing fancy, and do the above exercise.

Try it for five minutes for a week or two. Then, you can slowly increase that time incrementally to 7, 8, 9, 10, 15 minutes. What you will notice is that your thoughts begin to slow down. At first, you may have multiple thoughts going through your head at 100mph, but as you continue to allow them to float by, disintegrate, put them in a box or any combination thereof, they start to slow down, and you'll notice that there's space between them. Then more space between each one. This is a very effective technique I taught myself until I got to the point where there was so much space between thoughts, I actually startled myself and thought I was asleep (or dead!). You know that feeling when you're about to fall asleep and you suddenly gasp for air or jerk because you feel like you've completely surrendered. That may happen while meditating or when your alarm goes off telling you time is up. What you will also feel afterwards is more relaxed, less stressed, calm, refreshed and maybe even sleepy.

I first tried this during my lunch hour at work. I placed a note on my closed door that said, "do not disturb", silenced my phone, took my heels off, set an alarm, and it became my lunchtime ritual. If you want to deepen your practice even further, just add this one thing that's very powerful! As soon as you start and are seated doing the breathing, ensure your feet are touching the ground. Then, imagine your feet like they're the roots of a tree. Imagine the roots spreading outwards in the front and back of you, to the left and right of you, effortlessly grasping the carpet or floor underneath you. Feel grounded like a tree, with its roots deep in the soil.

There are so many benefits to meditating that many people do not realize. Perhaps the most fascinating to date is the scientific evidence that we can form new neural pathways in our brain called neuroplasticity. Scientific evidence shows that our brain has the ability to physically change by re-routing and recreating new connections in response to experiences.

> Based on environment, some of us may have a disposition to pain, trauma or negative neural pathways. ...In simple form, [to change this, is to change our] thought patterns, training our mind to ... add a positive [thought] to a negative or simply gain knowledge. (Liou, 2010)

> There are many different mechanisms of neuroplasticity ranging from the growth of new connections to the creation of new neurons. When the framework of neuroplasticity is applied to meditation, we suggest that the mental training of meditation is fundamentally no different than other forms of skill acquisition that can induce plastic changes in the brain. (Davidson & Lutz, 2010)

This is incredibly promising, especially in light of what we discussed in chapters two and three:

> We have pre-existing neural pathways we are so accustomed to unconsciously following...the power of pre-existing neural pathways are substantial. These pathways are created at a very young age; thus, continuously reinforced and strengthened, as the same information is being used and reaffirmed (Tassell, 2014). Cognitively, these pathways serve as the habitual "tape-recording" we play...Additionally, we can recognize heuristics (mental shortcuts) and their ability

to magnify the power of neural pathways, by proving how our brain can pull preconceived information forward like a shortcut (Goldstein, 2011). Since we can clearly see the power of strengthened and existing neural pathways, we can conversely ascertain their disappearance if we do not access such data often. If there is a long-term period where certain neural pathways are not used, they can completely dismantle. (Tassell, 2014)

Although our subconscious is at the forefront, guiding our thoughts and actions, we do have the ability to change our perceptions if we choose to. It's all about training the brain, or rather retraining the brain!

An interesting study was conducted in the U.S. at the urging of the Dalai Lama, after he gave a speech at the Society for Neuroscience's annual meeting in Washington, D.C. The Dalai Lama helped recruit Tibetan Buddhist monks for research on the brain and meditation in the Waisman Laboratory for Brain Imaging and Behavior at the University of Wisconsin-Madison.

The findings suggested that the cumulative practice of mediation had actually altered the structure and function of the Buddhist monks' brains, as assessed with functional magnetic resonance imaging (fMRI). Another study was conducted comparing meditation novices and experts. Those findings supported that those with extensive meditation training required minimal effort to sustain their focus and attention. Those expert meditators also showed less activation of their amygdala in comparison to the novices. The amygdala is the driver of our fight-flight response and is associated with our emotional responses of fear, stress, and aggression.

As Emily Fletcher so brilliantly shared: *"No one cares if you're good at meditation. Everyone cares if you're good at life: How kind are you? How present are you? How do you use your gifts to serve the world?" (2021).*

Storytime

I can personally attest to the power of meditating. It has completely regulated my nervous system (fight-flight response), which used to go from 0 to 100 in a matter of minutes whenever I was triggered. One of my biggest triggers was being disrespected and/or perceiving I was being disrespected. My physical body would have a reaction instantaneously (sensing danger/perceived danger). My heart would start racing, I would start breathing heavier, my jaw would clench, I would feel warmth around my neck, and my body may shake if the situation unfolded and became severe enough. I would literally feel my blood pressure rising. I didn't always have awareness as to what my body was doing. I just knew how I felt emotionally. It wasn't until I was seeing a relationship counselor with my boyfriend a few years ago that this was brought to my attention.

In the midst of one of my sessions, I was explaining a tumultuous incident my boyfriend and I had that week. In fact, I could barely wait to see the therapist that week to vent and process everything that had happened. Of course, as I was recounting the details during my appointment, I was reliving the incident all over again and getting all riled up. I knew and felt in the moment that I was getting emotionally "passionate" in my communications (code word for pissed AF!). We were about 20 minutes into our session when, to my surprise, in mid-sentence and heightened emotion, the therapist asked me to abruptly stop. He then curiously asked me about my arm and hand motions, which were still in mid-air, when I paused.

"What does it mean when your arms and hands do that?"

"Uhhhhh..." I replied, glancing down at my hands and arms.

"What is that?" he asked, attempting to copy my movements: elbows bent, fists clenched, pushing his forearms up and down. "If your arms were expressing an emotion, what would it be?"

Feeling a bit caught off guard and somewhat confused, I paused and replied: "FRUSTRATED!!"

"Do you always do that when you feel frustrated and you're talking?"

"I.........don't know. I never paid attention. But my hands feel really cold and numb right now."

"How about your breathing? You seem to be breathing kind of heavy..."

"Yeah, coz' I'm pissed!!!"

"How about your heart? How does your heart feel right now? Is it beating fast, hard, loud...what's it doing?"

"Umm. Yes, all of the above. I feel it pounding through my chest. I can literally see my blouse rising with each beat." (I'm thinking to myself: can we just get back to the story? I need to get this off my chest, LITERALLY!)

He nods, "Let's just sit here in silence for about five minutes. Ok, Cielo?"

Stunned and sitting there with my mouth slightly open, staring back at him, I reluctantly sat back in silence. So, now we are awkwardly sitting across each other, and he's quietly glancing around the room. So, I begin to do the same. Each time I glanced back at him, he was calmly sitting there with no facial expression. Just there. Looking around.

I didn't realize how long five minutes could feel. I sat there, a quiet observer. Time passed...slowly, but not in a bad way.

After the five minutes, he said: "How do you feel now?"

"Calm. Very relaxed. Almost sleepy, actually..." I said and began to yawn. (By the way, are you yawning right now reading this too? They say even reading the word "yawn" makes you yawn. I've yawned at least five times while typing this, so there must be some truth to it. Anyway, back to the story.)

He yawned too. (See?!) "Tell me how your body feels, Cielo?"

"Fine."

"No, tell me how your body feels. Let's start with your arms."

"My arms feel heavy, like dead weight on my lap. My legs, bottom, and back feel the pressure against the couch I'm sitting on. My hands feel warm. My heart is beating slow. I can barely notice it, in fact. My breathing is slow. My head and neck feel kind of heavy and like mush as they sit on my relaxed shoulders."

"Good, Cielo. What did you see...hear... feel...smell during those five minutes?"

"Well, as I looked around, I saw your bookcase. I looked at all the old books on the shelves. They were leaning over against one another, and they looked so peaceful. I wondered how long they had been there and when the last time they were picked up to be read was. I saw a film of dust on the shelf, and it seemed frozen in time. I was admiring the unique decorations on your wall and side table. They look like pieces from different parts of the world, and I wondered if you had traveled to these far-away places. I saw the plant in the corner, and its leaf was swaying as the air-conditioner blew on it from a distance. I heard the monotonous humming of the air-conditioner. I heard the squeaking of your chair when you shifted your body. I heard the faint background noise of your printer next to me. I heard the ticking from your clock on the table. I smelled the lingering scent of a candle that was likely lit earlier in the day. I smelled the fabric of the pillow I was clutching. I felt cool air brushing against my right lower leg. I felt my stomach growling, hungry for dinner. I felt the dryness in my mouth and throat."

"Excellent! Now, let's recall how you were feeling earlier before we took a pause."

(I chuckled) "Super heightened, hyper, upset, frustrated. My vitals were probably soaring. My mind was spinning. I couldn't talk fast enough to tell you everything I wanted to tell you."

"Yet despite how you were 'feeling' at that moment, your surroundings...this room...all those objects you mentioned, were exactly as is and perfectly still, weren't they? Even though your inner world felt crazy, unstable, chaotic...your outer world was perfectly peaceful, right?"

"Yes..."

"This peacefulness and stillness, Cielo, being in the present moment, is always available to you. Your feelings, at any given moment, are all internal. Even though you may 'feel' your world is turning upside down, you are only a few minutes away from coming back to this. The present. The reality of what's around you can also be within you."

(Mic drop!)

"What would your life be like if you learned that you are more powerful than you have ever been taught?"
— Bruce H. Lipton, PhD

WOW!! Talk about a life-changing, "A-HA" moment! That was the impetus of me paying attention to my body's manifestations of my thoughts and feelings: MINDFULNESS. I had no idea I had so much power over my nervous system. I used to have mini panic attacks in my earlier years whenever I would experience cumulative long-term stress. It would completely overwhelm my sensitive nervous system. I even broke out in chronic hives for a year and had to quit my job back in 2007. I had been a slave to my thoughts and reactions up until that session.

Now, I had an opportunity to form new neural pathways or reroute current ones in my brain. By inserting a new experience (practicing mindfulness) and changing the way my body reacted to stress, I could break an old, embedded pattern and literally change my life, and I did. I worked on my triggers the same exact way. By having awareness of what my triggers were, observing the pattern of my reactions when they occurred, breaking that pattern by doing something different (shifting my thoughts, shifting my behavior, shifting my actions) and repeating that over, and over, and over, and over again—then multiply that a few times, and finally, you free yourself! It is a lot of work, and it is painful work, but it's the most important work you will do.

If you'd like to try a simple and similar exercise on mindfulness, try this:

The Five Senses Exercise. The goal is to calm your mind by focusing on your environment rather than your thoughts. Take a couple of cleansing breaths, center yourself, then:

1) Notice five things that you can see. Glance around, in full awareness of your environment. Try to pick out five things that you wouldn't normally notice.

2) Notice four things you can feel. Perhaps it's the chair you are seated on, the table your arms are rested on, the fabric of the clothes you're wearing.

3) Notice three things that you can hear. Listen and notice things in the background that you wouldn't normally notice. Perhaps it's the humming of your air-conditioner, the birds chirping outside, the leaves of the tree brushing up against the window in the wind.

4) Notice two things you can smell. Perhaps it's the remnants of a cleaning agent used in your home, maybe it's the aroma in the kitchen, maybe it's the musty smell of your closet. Be aware of scents that you might typically filter out.

5) Notice one thing you can taste. Notice if there's a current taste in your mouth. Maybe chew a piece of gum or candy or take a sip of a drink.

As I attested with my own personal experience, this is very effective in calming yourself down when you are angry, feeling anxious, stressed or just want to relax and be present.

Gaëlle Desbordes, an instructor in radiology at (HMS) Harvard Medical School and a neuroscientist at (MGH's) Martinos Center for Biomedical Imaging, wanted to explore an alternative approach to treating depression (using) mindfulness-based meditation.

Studies have shown benefits against an array of conditions both physical and mental, including irritable bowel syndrome, fibromyalgia, psoriasis, anxiety, depression, and post-traumatic stress disorder... chronic pain...for patients engaging in a mindfulness meditation program, with effects similar to other existing treatments.

Researcher Gaelle Desbordes is probing mindfulness meditation's effect on depression, using functional magnetic resonance imaging (fMRI) to take before and after images of the brains of depressed patients who've learned to meditate. The work seeks to understand the internal brain processes affected by mindfulness meditation training in this population.

Desbordes' interest in the topic stems from personal experience. She began meditating as a graduate student in computational neuroscience at Boston University, seeking respite from the stress and frustration of academic life. Her experience convinced her that something real was happening to her and prompted her to study the subject more closely, in hopes of shedding enough light to underpin therapy that might help others.

'My own interest comes from having practiced those [meditation techniques] and found them beneficial, personally. Then, being a scientist, asking 'How does this work? What is this doing to me?' and wanting to understand the mechanisms to see if it can help others,' Desbordes said. 'If we want that to become a therapy or something offered in the community, we need to demonstrate [its benefits] scientifically.'

Desbordes' research uses functional magnetic resonance imaging (fMRI), which not only takes pictures of the brain, as a regular MRI does, but also records brain activity occurring during the scan. In 2012, she demonstrated that changes in brain activity in subjects who have learned to meditate hold steady even when they're not meditating. Desbordes took before-and-after scans of subjects who learned to meditate over the course of two months. She scanned them not while they were meditating, but while they were performing everyday tasks. The scans still detected changes in the subjects' brain activation patterns from the beginning to the end of the study...a part of the brain called the amygdala. (Powell, 2018)

Indeed, there are long-term beneficial effects of mindfulness and meditation, not only on our physical health but also our mental health. As it relates to using our using our gift of intuition:

"Intuition requires a deeper level of receptivity. It cannot operate when the mind is busy with other thoughts. A distracted mind can never be an intuitive mind."
— Unknown

Notes

_____

_____

_____

_____

_____

_____

_____

_____

_____

_____

_____

_____

_____

_____

_____

_____

It's ALL RIGHT!

"Intuition will tell the thinking mind where to look next."
— Jonas Salk

When it comes to intuition: It's ALL RIGHT. Let's talk anatomy:

The notion of left-sided or right-sided brain dominance is a widely accepted concept, although not "completely" validated or scientifically accepted in the context the layperson understands it to be. This theory first came to light in 1960 by Nobel Peace Prize winner Roger W. Sperry, a neuropsychologist who conducted split-brain experiments on how the brain's two hemispheres functioned differently.

The 1981 research was first conducted on cats and monkeys, and was later extended to epileptic patients who had undergone a procedure to separate the right and left hemispheres of the brain. It was during these studies that Sperry discovered a conscious mind exists in each hemisphere. The left-brain was dominant in language, arithmetic, analytical and verbal tasks, while the right-brain was superior in spatial comprehension, recognizing faces, understanding maps, and contributing to the emotional context of language. Sperry was quoted as saying: *"The great pleasure and feeling in my right brain is more than my left brain can find the words to tell you" (Roger Sperry, n.d.).*

From that came the widely accepted belief that the right and left brain could be characterized accordingly:

The left brain is more verbal, analytical, and orderly than the right brain. It's sometimes called the digital brain. It's better at things like reading, writing, and computations.

The left brain is also connected to:

logic	*mathematics*
sequencing	*facts*
linear thinking	*thinking in words*

The right brain is more visual and intuitive...It has a more creative and less organized way of thinking.

The right brain is also connected to:

imagination	*rhythm*
holistic thinking	*nonverbal cues*
intuition	*feelings visualization*
arts	*daydreaming*

He theorized that if you are mostly methodical and analytical in your thinking, you are left-brained. If you are more artistic and creative, you are right-brained. (Pietrangelo, 2019, para 8)

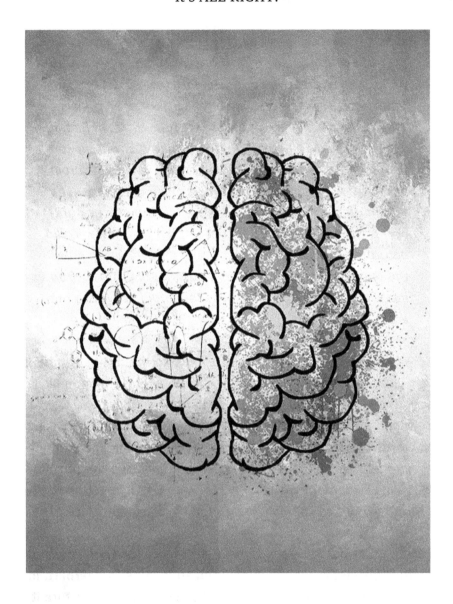

Senior Faculty Editor at Harvard Health Publishing, Robert H. Shmerling, MD shared his perspective on this:

There is truth to the idea that some brain functions reside more on one side of the brain than the other. We know this in part from what is lost when a stroke affects a particular part of the brain... But for more individual personality traits, such as creativity or a tendency toward the rational rather than the intuitive, there has been little or no evidence supporting a residence in one area of the brain. In fact, if you performed a CT scan, MRI scan, or even an autopsy on the brain of a mathematician and compared it to the brain of an artist, it's unlikely you'd find much difference...The notion of some people being more left-brained or right-brained is more a figure of speech than an anatomically accurate description...But, the lack of proof does not prove the opposite. For people living thousands of years ago, an inability to prove the earth was round did not prove the earth was flat! (2017)

So, there you have it! For simplicity, let's accept this right-brain/left-brain concept, and consider that the average person likely spends more time in his left brain on any given day by being logical, considering facts, analyzing, giving attention to details and thinking in words. We probably spend most of our waking and working hours there. But in life, everything is about balance. We do, after all, have two hemispheres. *"There is a voice that doesn't use words. Listen,"* says Rumi. The right brain seems like the right place to be!

Our intuition, our Superpower, has been silenced and overpowered by the constant competition and demands of its counterpart. In order for us to access and activate this gift, we must nurture it, exercise it, develop it, and attune to it. We are a society that is so busy doing, achieving, hustling instead of being, aligning, co-creating, manifesting and basking in our abundance. The latter does not imply sit still, do nothing and wish your desires into existence. Far from it. It's the realization that we've neglected the former, which is a beautiful and magical aspect of ourselves, a gift. It is a place of flow, grace, faith, submission and peace. It is a place of ease, yet not easy for most, at first. So, how can we tap into that right side of our brain? Well for one, we simply start using it. We need to make space in our lives to nurture this side of ourselves.

Storytime

Nine years ago in the midst of a major, difficult life transition (my divorce) and in an attempt to "find myself again", I decided to tap into my creative side and register for art classes at the Honolulu Museum of Art. I always had a creative mind but somehow lost this side of myself after years of being a military wife and mom and all the stressors that it comes with.

I enrolled in a watercolor class and on the first day, the instructor just asked us to play around and practice using the palette of colors and this special absorbent, textured paper. After piddle paddling around for a bit having created nothing but a series of blobs, drips and puddles, I decided I would be a bit more daring without instruction and use my pencil to draw pictures of butterflies, plants and flowers in an attempt to paint over it.

Well, I quickly learned that using this medium was unlike using acrylic or oil paint. It was very difficult to keep within the lines. I couldn't paint the details and patterns I envisioned in my head for the butterfly wings. Over and over again, I had to scrap my paintings and start over. I tried to use less water on my brush, tilt my paper to try to keep the water in the lines when it was bleeding out and blow on it to dry. I sat there sighing and trying so hard, getting frustrated. The instructor was making his rounds and strolled by each student. When he got to me, he stopped, hovered over my shoulder, saw my pile of scrapped "mistakes", smiled and whispered: "Stop trying to control it and see what happens."

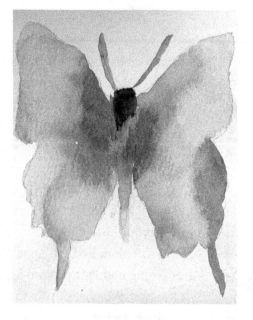

...and so, I took a deep breath and did just that. These were the results.

I learned how difficult it was to control watercolor. It did not like to be confined and forced to stay perfectly within the lines. The nature of watercolor is that it is just meant to flow. The beauty and essence of watercolor is in letting go of the need to control it. I allowed the color to bleed and branch out whichever way it wanted to go. I allowed it to be soft, fluid and flow with ease rather than forcing it to follow a certain pattern. The end result was something so original, beautiful and unexpected, all because I let go of the need to control it. Opportunities to learn life lessons are always around us, even in a watercolor class.

> *"The intellect has little to do on the road to discovery. There comes a leap in consciousness, call it intuition or what you will, and the solution comes to you and you don't know why or how."*
> — *Albert Einstein*

My new mantra: "Let go and be like watercolor."

What are your thoughts about things in your life that are outside of your control that you keep trying to control with your left brain? What would it feel like to let things go more easily and just flow?

Another way to tap into our right brain is to use a specific breathing technique during meditation called "Balancing Breath". It is a technique Emily Fletcher, founder of Ziva mediation, teaches based on the ancient technique used in yoga called Pranayama.

> *Prana means life force or breath sustaining the body; Ayama translates as "to extend or draw out." In the yoga tradition, the breath is said to carry a person's life force. In Traditional Chinese Medicine, Energy or QI — pronounced "chee" — is the essential life force that flows through all of nature. This Energy is the vitality that gives life and direction to all matter. We believe that a balanced movement of QI has the power to strengthen, energize and heal the body. (Reed & Gramly, 2021)*

Unlike the technique we discussed in the former chapters of, "Two second inhales through the nose and four second exhales through the mouth," you are actually going to alternate breathing through the right and left nostrils, depressing one as you move back and forth to the other. It would look like this:

Seated in a comfortable position with your back supported and your head free, we are going to use your thumb and ring finger.

1. Lightly hover your hand over your mid-face/nose area about an inch or two away from your face.

2. Now, take your thumb and close your right nostril. Exhale through your left nostril, then inhale.

3. Then, switch. Close your left nostril with your ring finger and exhale and inhale through the right.

Repeat back and forth for about five full cycles. This is going to feel a bit weird at first as you awkwardly get the hang of it. Ensure your inhales are all the way to full. When you reach that peak at the top, there's a little space there to transition and effortlessly switch and allow your exhale to empty from your lungs slowly. Notice there's a tiny space in that exhale at the bottom. Allow that breath to simply fill back up into your lungs as you inhale. Do this at your own pace, taking your time. In doing this technique, it is stimulating the right and left hemispheres of the brain at the same time (Fletcher, 2005). The right and left hemispheres have a bridge that connects them, called the corpus callosum. This thick bundle of nerve fibers ensures that both sides of the brain can communicate and send signals to each other. Including this Balancing Breath technique as part of your meditation practice makes it that much more powerful.

Meditation has proven to strengthen the corpus callosum. Numerous scientific studies have shown a link between long-term meditation practices and the structure of the corpus callosum. They were larger in long-term meditators compared to control subjects, likely indicating greater connectivity and increased hemispheric integration during cerebral processes. There was also a positive correlation in brain asymmetry that had occurred from years of meditation, suggesting changes in attention processing, as we previously discussed with the research they did with the Tibetan monks.

So, if you are new to meditation, you can try the Balancing Breath technique as a stand-alone or a pre-cursor to delving into your practice. You can find a video of Emily Fletcher demonstrating this on her YouTube channel: Ziva Meditation, "The Balancing Breath".

The more you access and exercise your right brain, the closer you are to your intuitive mind.

"The intuitive mind is where our genius resides."
— A. Artemis

Notes

Soul Goals

"You don't have a soul. You are a soul. You have a body."
— *CS Lewis*

Let's fully grasp this concept:

We've learned from chapter one that we are not just our physical body. We learned in chapter two that we are not our subconscious mind (imposter). In chapter three, we learned that we are not our actions and behaviors (programming, which stems from our triggers, trauma, and past). We just learned in chapter four that we are not our thoughts either. Well, if we aren't all those things, then who or what the heck are we?

YOU. ARE. A. SOUL.

We are first and foremost a soul or a spirit (many use those terms interchangeably and that's perfectly fine. No need to get into semantics). The bottom line is we are way more than what we deem ourselves to be. One of the barriers that prevent people from exploring this part of themselves is they think it is religious-based or about organized religion. As I stated in chapter one, this is about spirituality versus religion. Spirituality is a sense of connection to something bigger than ourselves. For some, like myself, that is "God" and for others, it's "The Universe", "Source", "Spirit", "Cosmos", "Creation", or "Mother Earth". Let's not define what it is exactly by boxing it into religion or anything else. This is where our ego gets in the way; it causes us to think that other people's beliefs are either right or wrong based on our own beliefs and agendas. Being a spiritual being is about inclusivity, not exclusivity. I want you to think of your soul as your "Higher Self". It is all-knowing and has all the answers within. It connects you to higher realms of human understanding and limitations. This realization that you are part of this whole, WE are all part of this whole, is the key to fully developing and mastering your intuition.

This is a realm that goes beyond your five senses, your human experience. This is where our intuition is unlocked. It is not enough, however, to just unlock it. What good is it to have a key if we are not going to use it to open something and step through? You ever have a junk drawer or a keychain full of random keys? At some point, you want to clean up your junk drawer or your heavy keyring that's weighing down your purse or pocket by figuring out what key goes with what lock. If they are random, unpaired keys, at some point, we will throw them away. It's pointless to have a key that doesn't open anything, right? The same goes with your door to intuition. I'm handing you the key to unlock it, but it's up to you to step through. Here's the thing: everything happens in Divine or synchronized timing. There are no coincidences. (More on this in later chapters). Some of you may read this book and begin eagerly practicing its contents; some of you may not pick up or read this book for months, years, or maybe never at all. Maybe you end up gifting it to someone else. Whatever the situation, it is exactly as it is supposed to be.

Storytime

I once had a roommate who loaned me a book by Paulo Coelho called "The Alchemist". It had sat on top of my nightstand for over six months collecting dust. Believe it or not, I'm not much of a reader. In fact, I can count on one hand how many books I've read from front to back in my lifetime. Quite the irony since you're now reading a book I authored. The truth of the matter is, most of the time I would fall asleep and never finish reading. Perhaps the author's writing wasn't as riveting as the one you are reading now. (Insert hysterical laughter here! I'm literally cracking myself up!) The same goes for movies. I'm infamous for falling asleep and then waking up several times, rewinding and asking, "What happened, what happened?" I even tried listening to audiobooks. To prevent me from falling asleep, I used to listen to them on my long drive to work on the freeway, but then I'd find myself daydreaming and having to rewind the audio. Anyway, I totally digressed. The point was, there is a method and madness to universal timing.

I was in the middle of packing for a trip to Vegas when I happened to glance over at that dusty book that had been on my nightstand for six months. It's as if it waved me down from the corner of my eye. It was partially covered under a tissue box, and all I could see was the author's name: Paulo Coelho. It was a fairly thin book and looked like a perfect read for my six-hour flight to Vegas, so I dusted it off and into my carry-on bag it went. It was an evening flight, and there I sat with the lights dimmed. I wasn't quite sleepy yet, so I decided to whip out the book, certain it would be the perfect tranquilizer, per usual. Fast-forward six hours later, the plane's wheels touched ground in Vegas, and my eyes were peeled to the book, reading the last pages. While everyone disembarked, I sat in my empty row, finishing up the final page, and my life was changed forever. The timing of my reading it was impeccable for what I was going through in my life at that point. I had been going through deep healing, lots of pain and suffering, a loss of self, a loss in faith that had been triggered by heartache after heartache and failed relationships—the "Dark Night of the Soul", as it were. I was doing the inner work through the pain, and this little book called out to me at just the right time. I was in the midst of my spiritual awakening and didn't even know what that was...

The "Spiritual Awakening" marks the beginning of our spiritual path. It is a journey of transformation back to "self": your soul self, your authentic self, your Higher Self. It can be likened to the metamorphosis of a butterfly. We can all appreciate the sighting of a beautiful butterfly, but do we truly realize what it had to endure to transform into that end-state?

The Caterpillar Stage

In this stage of the butterfly's life (which follows right after hatching from an egg) the main task is consumption. The caterpillar's purpose is simply to eat as much as possible in order to fuel the growth that will take place in the future. During this stage, the caterpillar will outgrow and shed its skin as many as four or five times.

The Chrysalis Stage

This is the most intriguing stage of butterfly development, which appears catastrophic from the perspective of the caterpillar. When the little crawler is fully grown and can eat no more, it simply dangles from a branch and spins a protective cocoon around itself so it can safely rest and digest all the food that has been consumed in the previous stage. Though the chrysalis appears unchanged from the outside during this stage, there is a dramatic transformation taking place inside. The body of the caterpillar is slowly dissolving while the previously dormant precursor cells of the emerging butterfly gradually develop, migrate together and create a brand-new being.

The Butterfly Stage

At last, in this final stage, the fully developed butterfly is ready to emerge from the chrysalis. After breaking free, the butterfly's wings are still folded and wet and more rest time is necessary to allow blood to flow into the wings. Finally, when the unfurled wings are fully dry, the butterfly is ready to take flight and share its beauty with the world.

During this stage there is an intentional "breaking free" that has to occur with proper timing before "flight" is undertaken. (Wyatt, 2015)

Like the butterfly, before our spiritual awakening, we are in a state of spiritual slumber: a "spiritual coma". Everything you have read in this book up until this point is part of that awakening process. Our patterns and programming will repeat until they're healed. Until then, we live life mindlessly asleep. We remain stuck, unevolved, and limited in our life. We pass this down to our children, grandchildren, and generations thereafter. It is part of the journey to emerge into a whole new you, which, in essence, is returning to your authentic self. Before you ever came into this world, before you were ever programmed, before you handed over control of your mind and emotions, and before you ever self-identified or overly identified with your ego. The "Dark Night of the Soul" is about ego death, so you can spiritually awaken your soul. It is our soul's cry to spiritually awaken and go through this metamorphosis. By the way, do you remember what the images were that I painted in my watercolor class in the previous chapter?

This chapter delves more into the ego, the "I", and clearly differentiating it from your soul. The goal is to know when you are in ego versus your soul self. That is where the proverbial rubber meets the road in your transformation. In chapter three, I gave the analogy of the ego being the anti-virus software to your computer. Your computer (subconscious mind) is constantly running its programming (adopted beliefs, experiences, memories) in the background. The anti-virus software (ego) is constantly filtering information that's being received by your conscious mind and rejects any foreign or suspicious data to protect the computer and its programming.

Now, if you're not very techy, you may appreciate another example as a frame of reference. So, let me offer you this as well:

I want you to think of your subconscious mind like an old, historic family mansion that was handed down from generations and generations of family lineage. It has antiques, family heirlooms and prized possessions in there. This mansion has a protective barrier around it: a massive, sturdy steel gate. You have top-notch security guarding the entrance and only allow family through. Everyone else is deemed a stranger and possible threat. Use your imagination with whatever security you want to envision. Maybe it's like the queen's guards at Buckingham Palace in England. Maybe it's a Marine with a massive weapon draped over his chest standing dead center in front of the gate with a look that could kill you. Maybe it's a vicious dog behind the gate that is snarling and growling, saliva dripping, pacing back and forth on high alert ready to eat someone alive at the thought of coming near its entrance. Maybe it's one or a combination thereof (I'll personally take the Marine: "Oorah!"). Whichever one of those appeals to you, that protective security to your mansion (subconscious mind), which houses all those prized family heirlooms and possessions (programmed beliefs, memories, experiences), is called your ego. That security system (ego) will screen any visitors coming through. It is hypervigilant for intruders and will protect your mansion and everything inside at all costs.

Your ego is the voice and defender of your subconscious mind. It believes it's keeping you safe and protecting you from external threats (perceived external threats, that is) but in actuality, it's keeping you from experiencing reality:

The ego is always on guard against any kind of perceived diminishment. Automatic egorepair mechanisms come into effect to restore the mental form of 'me'. When someone blames or criticizes me, that to the ego is a diminishment of self, and it will immediately attempt to repair its diminished sense of self through self-justification, defense, or blaming. Whether the other person is right or wrong is irrelevant to the ego. It is much more interested in self-preservation than in the truth. This is the preservation of the psychological form of 'me.' Even such a normal thing as shouting something back when another driver calls you 'idiot' is an automatic and unconscious egorepair mechanism. One of the most common ego-repair mechanisms is anger, which causes a temporary but huge ego inflation. All repair mechanisms make perfect sense to the ego but are actually dysfunctional. (Tolle, 2008)

The ego prevents you from recognizing itself because it is part of your subconscious mind. Instead, it always wants to point to those outside of itself, clearly seeing the flaws and faults of others. It forms judgements and opinions that are misinterpreted as "truth", when in reality, it creates its own experience, yet is blind to its own dysfunction. From a spiritual perspective, the ego is the "veil" that is covering our eyes. Thus, why it's referred to as the "false self" versus your "Higher Self".

Ego vs. Spirit

Ego	Spirit
Needs to control the situation	Flows + trusts Divine timing
Views life as a competition	Celebrates everyone's success
Struggles	Aligns
Fear-based Lives in past + worries for the future	Centered Lives in present moment +open to possibilities
Operates from lack	Abundance mentality

THE EGO

false self

Self-betrayal
Me
Separation
Blame
Angry
Resentment
Fear
Complains
Envious
Intolerance
Power-seeking
Materialism
Reactive
Chaos
Self-righteous
Doing
Complexity

THE SOUL

true self

Self-love
We
Unity
Accountability
Joyful
Forgiveness
Love
Grateful
Supportive
Tolerance
Power within
Minimalism
Responsive
Peace
Humble
Being
Simplicity

False Self Ego	True Self Soul
victim mentality	takes responsibility for creating one's experience
judgmental/critical	accepting/respectful of others
focused on past or future	present focused
keeps conflict and drama alive	forgiving; stays away from drama
feels superior or inferior to others	knows we are all equal
feels alone in the world	knows we are all connected and part of Source
stressed and worried about the future	flows, trusts, manifests
proves worth through work or service	knows one's worth and value are not based on external accomplishments
takes self too seriously	able to laugh at oneself
insecure	secure
ruled by time	trusts in the flow of Life
seeks approval from others	confident in own self
doesn't like to be alone unless distracted	comfortable with oneself
attention and validation seeking	humble and secure with own abilities
unconscious	conscious

Some common examples of ego patterns:

- Taking things personally or being easily offended
- Feeling you are right, and others are wrong
- Judging, blaming, criticizing, accusing, complaining
- Giving your unsolicited opinion or advice
- Being overly concerned with how people see you
- Needing to have enemies
- Making things about "you". Always talking about your problems, making a scene, everything revolves around or somehow goes back to "you"
- Demanding attention to yourself and getting upset if recognition is not given
- Applying negative labels to people
- Using your possessions, knowledge, status, physical looks to impress others
- Bringing about temporary ego inflation through angry reactions against someone or something
- Wanting to be seen as or appear important

"The simplest definition of ego is it destroys everything in its path" — *(Unknown).* This is especially true of our relationships with one another.

Wow, the ego just sounds like a horrific part of who we are, doesn't it? I used to think that too. But if we think about it, the ego developed simply to protect the family heirlooms and prized possessions within—our identity. It was just doing its job. Even in our healing, it serves a purpose. Without it, we wouldn't have a point of reference, a contrast, to discern our growth. Think of the ego as your amigo. Befriend it, for it continues to serve a purpose. Embrace it, accept it, own it, and witness it. Thank it for doing its job. Comfort it when you realize it is repeating old patterns. Remind it that it works as a team in harmony alongside your spirit. It is a part of you. It will always be there. In our daily life, if we can learn to pause, instead of react, our spirit will guide us to clarity. This is why we must be diligent about spending more time with our spirit.

You'll notice as you practice witnessing ego stories, that the ego does this nearly every moment of every day. As we practice, we can get beyond our own ego stories and respond in new ways. We can get to the core of our reactions. We can become curious, conscious and have more grace towards ourselves and others. (LePera, 2020)

Eventually, the voice of our ego will soften to a mere whisper, and you'll step into the truth of who you are. This is a place of **inner peace** instead of giving someone a **piece of your mind** because the former is not dependent on other people or your surroundings. This is a place of consciously **responding** instead of furiously **reacting**. This is a place of **empowerment** instead of feeling **powerless** over the things you can't control. This is a place of **gratitude** instead of having an **attitude.** This is a place of **detachment** instead of **attachment.** This is a place of **inclusivity** instead of **exclusivity.** This is the place your soul-self resides...and out of the cocoon emerges the beautiful butterfly. Alas, you've transformed into your Higher Self.

Notes

Come to Your Senses!

Like a cell phone tower that receives signals with its antennas, you have this capability too. You don't need a carrier like Verizon, Sprint, AT&T; you are the carrier and have direct access. Or better yet, you ARE the cell tower. However, as we previously discussed, we all tend to be so busy hustling, in our ego self, that we are detached from the full capabilities of our antennas and all the signals it receives from our five senses.

There is a whole other level of the spiritual realm that we haven't yet experienced. Perhaps we've taken our senses for granted, and it isn't until we experience a loss of one of them that we can fully appreciate the experiences and fullness they bring to our lives. Just think about how hard it would be to get around if someone blindfolded you. How unsatisfying it would be to eat a delicious, savory, hot meal without the ability to smell or taste it. How limiting it would feel to not be able to kiss, touch, hold and hug your loved ones and resort to a telephone call or zoom, skype or Facetime like we've had to do through COVID. All these things take away from the full experience, don't they? It helps us to realize how important it is to have all our senses engaged to fully experience the beauty of life's moments.

While the five give us information about what is external to our bodies, we have additional sense receptors that provide information about our own bodies, internally. Depending on which source you cite, you will find data that states we actually have anywhere from 8 to 14 to 22 to 33 "senses"!

Sensory systems are widespread throughout the body including those that detect the world directly from the outside (exteroreceptors), those that detect information from internal organs and processes (interoceptors), and those detecting sense of position and load (proprioception) (Marzvanyan 2020).

These receptors all over our body communicate with us daily.

Exteroceptors – include the five senses as well as other skin sensations such as pressure, superficial pain, temperature, itching, and tickling.

Interoceptors – help us understand our body's inner sensations from our internal organ functions like heart rate, body temperature, hunger, thirst, digestion, respiration, blood pressure, urinary system, autonomic nervous system as well as chemical stimuli, pain stimuli and the state of our emotions. Some examples would be having a full bladder and needing to go to the bathroom, feeling angry and your heart races and your face feels flush, feeling stuffed from having eaten too much, or your stomach grumbling from being hungry.

Proprioceptors – occur deep beneath the skin in the skeletal muscles, tendons, ligaments, and joints. Also includes body positioning—senses of movement, vibration, position, and balance. For example, this is what allows us to close our eyes and point our finger to our nose or step off a bus and know where to land your foot or ring a doorbell and control how hard you press it with your fingers.

Honestly, I'm a little offended that my 'sense of humor' wasn't captured in that list. Moving on...

We are all experiencing these senses, and they work collaboratively, although much in our world has contributed to our lack of awareness and connection to our own body, such as distractions with technology, masking symptoms with medications, and taking our bodies for granted and working it like a horse or simply avoiding its whispers. I would like for you to start thinking of your body as having its own voice, because it does, and it speaks to you. But we must truly listen and honor it, in order to interpret what it's trying to convey. After all, the ability to use our intuition is to go from sensation(s) to perception (receiving, integrating then interpreting), and it starts with our own bodies. Our mind, body, and spirit are all connected.

Outside of this, we must also consider all the other things in this world that we are not even picking up on like our furry friends do. If you've had a pet, you know they react to things we can't even detect, whether that's through their sense of smell, feeling some type of vibration through the ground or negative energy in the room. We've heard of pets barking, whining and displaying strange and unusual behavior, especially right before things like earthquakes, tsunamis or thunderstorms. Even though, as humans, we also have the sense of vibration, we are not as attuned to it as our furry counterparts. For one, we don't have direct contact with the ground much anymore, as animals do. We always have shoes and clothing on. We are more focused on what's around us like other people, other sights, and other sounds.

Other animals have the ability to detect the Earth's magnetic fields (magnetoreception), which comes from the flow of molten material in the earth's core and the flow of ions in the Earth's atmosphere generating a magnetic field that surrounds the planet. Detecting this is useful in providing a sense of direction. In fact, for many years, researchers thought that this ability only existed in migratory birds, fish and a few other animals. However, a study conducted in March 2019 on human magnetoreception, published in the journal of eNeuro, may have proved otherwise. In this study, participants were placed in a small chamber surrounded by a small, manmade magnetic field. The EEG machine placed on their heads showed brain activity similar to when the brain is stimulated by light and sound. Although capturing this implied our brain responds to magnetic fields, researchers are not quite clear what that means yet.

Although many migrating and homing animals are sensitive to Earth's magnetic field, most humans are not consciously aware of the geomagnetic stimuli that we encounter in everyday life. Either we have lost a shared, ancestral magnetosensory system, or the system lacks a conscious component with detectable neural activity but no apparent perceptual awareness by us. Given the known presence of highly evolved geomagnetic navigation systems in species across the animal kingdom, it is perhaps not surprising that we might retain at least some functioning neural components especially given the nomadic hunter/gatherer lifestyle of our not-too-distant ancestors. The full extent of this inheritance remains to be discovered. (Wang & Hilburn, 2019)

The human eye can detect light of only certain wavelengths (from violet to red), but butterflies and bees can detect ultraviolet light and snakes can see infrared light. The human range for hearing is commonly given as 20 to 20,000 Hz. Several animal species produce and detect sounds well beyond what humans can detect and over a wide range of frequencies. For example, bats and dolphins can hear upwards of 100,000 Hz. They use ultrasound/sound waves to "see", navigate and capture prey. On the other end of the spectrum are whales who can hear infrasonic sounds as low as 7 Hz.

Animal hearing frequency range

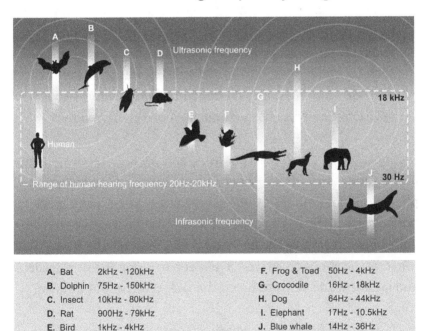

A. Bat	2kHz - 120kHz	F. Frog & Toad	50Hz - 4kHz
B. Dolphin	75Hz - 150kHz	G. Crocodile	16Hz - 18kHz
C. Insect	10kHz - 80kHz	H. Dog	64Hz - 44kHz
D. Rat	900Hz - 79kHz	I. Elephant	17Hz - 10.5kHz
E. Bird	1kHz - 4kHz	J. Blue whale	14Hz - 36Hz

We humans can only sense a fraction of what is truly out there. There are frequencies that are inaudible to us, yet they are emitted all around us. But perhaps the most important of all frequencies that we must attune to is that of Mother Earth herself.

The "heartbeat" of Mother Earth is the frequency of 7.83 Hz, also known as the "Schumann Resonance" (named after physicist Dr. Winfried Otto Schumann who discovered this back in 1952). Interestingly, 7.83 hertz is also the human brain's average alpha/theta brainwave frequency. As you recall from the previous chapter, alpha/theta brainwave frequency induces deep levels of relaxation, meditation, hypnosis as well deep levels of enhanced creativity, insight, and inspiration.

> One of the main researchers on this topic, Dr. Wolfgang Ludwig, discovered that while the Earth's vibration could be clearly measured in nature and in the ocean, it was almost impossible to measure it in the city, where manmade signals such as radios, TVs, cars, buildings, phones, and the like override natural signals. He began thinking that this could have large implications on human well-being. (Guzman, 2017)

Technology has taken over our lives, and we are literally plugged in and saturated with Wi-Fi (inside and outside of our homes), cell phones, and countless other electronics that we even wear on our physical bodies. Is it too far-fetched to think we have become imbalanced from the Earth's natural electromagnetic frequency? What ramifications could this have? People feeling stressed, anxious and imbalanced seems to be on the rise. What about disease?

> If RF (radio frequency) radiation is absorbed by the body in large enough amounts, it can produce heat. This can lead

to burns and body tissue damage. Although RF radiation is not thought to cause cancer by damaging the DNA in cells the way ionizing radiation does, there has been concern that in some circumstances, some forms of non-ionizing radiation might still have other effects on cells that might somehow result in cancer.

Cell phones and cell phone towers (base stations) use RF radiation to transmit and receive signals. Some concerns have been raised that these signals might increase the risk of cancer, and research in this area continues. (ACS, 2020)

It's not far-fetched. It's concerning that we may not know the true impact for years to come. A recent study, however, has some promising news in that they found, *"The Schumann resonance frequency of 7.83 Hz can inhibit the growth of (certain) cancer cells and that using a specific frequency type can lead to more effective growth inhibition" (Tang et al., 2019).* The Earth's vibrational frequency is a binaural beat, meaning that the right and left ear each receive a slightly different frequency tone, yet the brain perceives these as a single tone.

Binaural beats have been found to be extremely healing and beneficial for grounding, stability, and overall well-being. In fact, a 2019 study found a significant link between prolonged exposure to binaural beats and a reduction in anxiety. Binaural beat therapy is an emerging form of sound therapy for this reason. It can be used for both relaxation, meditative purposes or if the binaural beats are increased in their frequency to match the beta state of 13-30 Hz, it can increase focus, alertness, motivation and concentration.

The proverbial, "There's so much more than meets the eye," could not be any truer. Or in this case, there's so much more **than** our senses. There's so much more **to** our senses. There's so much more that we are **not** sensing, and so much more we may be **sensitive** to. Make **sense**? Perfect segue to chapter eight...

Notes

Notes

More CLAIR-ITY

"Everything in Life is Vibration." – Albert Einstein

You are ENERGY! Everything is ENERGY!

> *Wherever there is space, time, energy, or matter, there is an electromagnetic field, and this field is "the life force." The life force, mind, soul, spirit, consciousness – these things exist in the Universe, and they are part of physics. Therefore, a physics of the human spirit is possible. The standard EKG and EEG taken within western medicine only scratch the surface of the science of human energy fields. (Ross, 2009, p 5)*

We all have a **life force** that flows through us, and it affects our health, mood, and vitality! In Chinese and Japanese culture, it is referred to as ki or qi (pronounced chee). In India, it is known as prana (breath/vital force/power). It is the energy that spins and flows through our chakras/energy centers/energy wheels, located from the base of our spine to the crown of our head.

If you've ever had acupuncture and wondered how sticking those long, skinny needles in various places in your body helps heal pain, headaches and various illnesses, it is this very life force that they are working with. Traditional Chinese medicine uses acupuncture as a technique for balancing the flow of energy or life force. The insertion of needles is carefully placed along the meridians that flow throughout your body. This can be somewhat likened to blood vessels in our physical body, but they are energetic instead. Energy in your body flows through this channel. When a blockage or imbalance occurs, it can manifest as a physical or emotional issue, and eventually, pain or illness can ensue. It's important to get back to a place of balance.

If you've ever had energy work by any Energy Healing Practitioner, we channel energy through our hands, acting as a conduit, to help move any stuck or stagnant energy in your chakras/energy centers and through your body as a whole to facilitate its rebalance. There's so much that our bodies store in the form of energy, most of which has to do with past emotional traumas, which affect our physical body and health. Most people are completely oblivious to this.

Storytime

For most people, energy work is actually very relaxing, and people often fall asleep. When I first tried healing energy work for myself (before I ever became a practitioner), I felt the energy actually run through me. WHAT?!? It's true! Not in a bad, painful way, but it was actually strong enough for my body to jerk and jolt. Kind of like when you feel really cold, need a jacket and get that "brrrr", shivering, shaky feeling. Yet inside, I felt really calm, relaxed, almost meditative. I always knew I was energy-sensitive, but in the way that I could see subtleties in situations and people that most wouldn't. I also knew I picked up other people's energy, as I would get drained or overstimulated. But, I never experienced energy in that visceral way until then. Quite fascinating. It would be the beginning of the expansion of God's plans for me and further open up my intuitive gifts as a healer.

I have had many female clients come to me for healing. After a while, I noticed a commonality with those that had blockages or imbalances in their sacral chakra. This is the energy center located in the pelvic area, below the belly button. This chakra deals with our emotional states, our creativity, our sexuality, relationships, reproduction, and is also considered the mother womb or what I like to call "mother wound". Any manifestation of emotional blockages would show up in the physical body as ailments in the reproductive area, lower back, or abdominal area. In 100% of the cases I have assisted, the women who had female "dis-ease" such as endometriosis, polycystic ovary syndrome (PCOS), fertility issues, and more of the like, had a history of sexual trauma and/or deep emotional trauma related to their mother. In 100% of the cases, they never revealed anything to me in advance. In fact, most of the time, they came to me for another reason: anxiety, depression, feeling imbalanced, they were "just curious", always wanted to try, felt pulled emotionally and energetically to see me, or a series of "coincidences" brought them to me somehow.

When I started doing energy work on them, as they lay on their backs with their eyes closed, my hands were led to hover about five inches over their pelvic area. I would notice a change in temperature in comparison to other parts of their body as I was slowly gliding my hands over. This typically feels like warmth in the area that needs healing. I was drawn to channel healing energy here to break strongholds. This would present itself as certain imagery in my spiritual eyes (third eye). It might come in the form of patterning and texture, or darker shades of color in the cells, tissues, organs, and energy center themselves. I would have a knowing that prayer and love needed to be channeled there. Sometimes I would feel led to remove or extract energy. I have had sessions where the client would suddenly break out in tears, yet couldn't see or know what I was doing as their eyes were closed. They just felt a wave of emotions come over them. It's a release of the stuck emotions, the pain.

Each of us is so very empowered to heal our own selves, emotionally and physically, if we can step into this spiritual space, fully submit, and honor the voice of our own bodies. I simply offer my intuition, my intuitive gifts, my prayers, and my hands as a channel to help promote this in someone. First, to help them realize what is energetically happening in their body, followed by supporting, encouraging, and empowering them through counsel and prayer. I have had many amazing clients make life-changing shifts, emotionally, mentally, physically, and spiritually. All the glory be to God because He is who I channel all my healing energy from.

Because we are energetic beings, each of us is picking up, exchanging, and giving away energy all day every day. You have likely already sensed this when someone gets too close to you and violates your personal space. You may feel a need to step back or ask the other person to move back to create a comfortable space that feels safe. This is because we are multidimensional beings. In fact, we have a total of seven "subtle bodies" or energetic layers, that vibrate at different frequencies which make up our aura. Our aura extends out from our body like an outline, kind of like a halo, but it is rays of vibrant colors. It is our energy that emits outwardly, anywhere from about one to three feet. Our aura can tell a lot about our current state. The brighter our aura, the more love, joy, and genuine positivity we possess and exude. The dimmer or darker it is, the lower the frequency of emotions we carry, such as hate, negativity, resentment, despair, regret, anxiety, etc. Our aura is impacted by stressors such as illness as well, or simply our lack of self-care.

We also pick up energies from others that can make us feel drained, anxious, or just out of sorts. Have you ever walked into a room and immediately felt the energy? Or perhaps you're the one inside the room and someone else walks in and shifts the energy. Whether it was a good vibe or a bad vibe, what you were sensing is the frequency of their energy. The higher the vibration, the more positive it feels. The lower the vibration the more negative it feels.

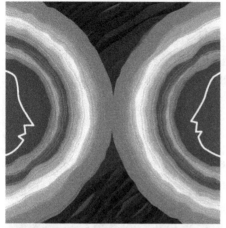

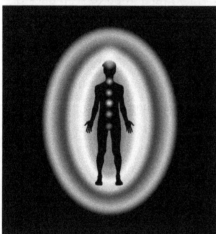

Our aura is an extension of our energy centers/chakras from the base of the spine to the top of our head/crown.

Each chakra corresponds to an inner organ or gland in our physical body that affects our health and vitality.

Chakras distribute life force throughout our body. From top to bottom:

Crown
Third eye
Throat
Heart
Solar Plexus
Sacral
Root

Have you ever been around someone and it just feels so good to be in their company? It's like they're a breath of fresh air and you just immediately feel uplifted in their presence. You may not even be able to pinpoint exactly what it is—maybe they're fun, they smile a lot, they're positive, they care, they're kind, they're genuine, and they light up a room, so to speak. Well, in essence, they really are! What you are experiencing is someone of a higher frequency. Like tends to attract like, but also be aware, people with higher frequencies also tend to attract those with lower vibrations.

Similarly, those with lower vibrations gravitate towards them as well. It's because they need that positive, uplifting energy. It can be an unconscious or conscious energy exchange. Lower vibration can come about from illness or depression or it can be personality-driven. Someone who always finds something to complain about. They're constantly in a state of victimhood and negativity. You may have a friend, family member, or co-worker that calls on you for support or "to vent" (aka vomit) about their life. By the time they're done, they feel a huge weight lifted, yet you feel completely exhausted and may even walk away with a headache! YIKES! It's up to us to hold energetic boundaries. If you are a sensitive person like me (empath or highly sensitive person), you need to be extra cautious and discerning about who you expend your energy on. Sensitives are like lint rollers who pick up everything and take it on as their own, like a transference of energy if you will.

Being intuitive is about learning how to tune into energy and frequencies, and not just what is 10 to 20 feet in front of you. We can begin to do this most accurately when we first get to know ourselves more intimately in body, mind, and spirit. We now have the information and tools to do that from each chapter that preceded this. We now have so much awareness, the veil has been lifted, we have expanded our mind, our senses, and now our energy. It is said that a mind that it stretched can never go back to its old dimensions. We are now multi-dimensional—in mind and body—so let us keep exploring spirit and gain more CLAIR-ity!

"The Clairs", as they are called, is a special intuitive ability that uses our five senses. Remember back in the day when we had dial radios? You'd have to move that knob left and right, hearing static until you get to juuuuust the right spot to pick up on a radio station playing music. (Please tell me you know what I'm talking about, and

I didn't just date myself using that example!) Annnywaaay, clair-ly, I better just move on!

The Clairs correspond with our five senses and how spirit communicates with us on an intuitive level. We typically have one or two dominant ones that just come naturally to us and our strong suit. God/Spirit will choose that which is easiest for us to connect. All the Clairs can be unlocked and developed in due time. There are no limits, and all ways of receiving are truly a blessing.

Clairvoyance means clear seeing.
In our mind's eye or third eye, we receive images in the form of pictures and symbols, as if we were watching bits of a movie trailer or daydreaming. It can also come in during meditation or in your sleep and you will have a vivid recollection of it upon waking. They can come during waking hours or sleep state or both. If you are a visual learner and do best when ideas are in images or written format, then your dominant gift may be clairvoyance. Also, pay attention to what your passions and interests may be and if they tend to use the sense of sight creatively, such as photography, art or design.

Clairaudience means clear hearing.
This spiritual ability allows you to hear Spirit's communications and guidance like your own inner voice. Kind of like what it sounds like when you're silently reading the words in a book. We may also hear the voice of a loved one who has passed when we are in a light dream state. What you hear can be internal or external. Maybe you hear a bible verse or a preacher's sermon that speaks to you at just the right time. Some possibilities that this Clair may be your dominant one: you may experience buzzing or ringing in your ears (not related to a medical diagnosis) that make your hearing more

sensitive. You may have an aversion to loud music or loud places. Your learning style may be best through hearing. You may have "an ear for music", songwriting, or singing. You may have songs that tend to get stuck in your head. You may have a tendency to think out loud and talk to yourself.

Clairsentience means clear feeling.
Often referred to as the sixth sense or your intuition. It is the ability to clearly feel and sense energy, especially people's emotional states and often their physical states too. We can gather information from all living or non-living things as well, without the use of any other senses. This may also come in the form of goosebumps or what I like to call "God bumps" for myself. Whenever I am coaching someone, reading for someone or just having a conversation with anyone and I start to give them advice or minister to them in some way, I begin to feel God bumps in my arms, which tells me that the message is coming from Spirit. It's a "word" they need to hear. I will often just instinctively say, "This message is for you." It comes out in an effortless flow, and I feel that I'm hitting a nerve with that person.

Most empaths are clairsentients as they can sense and feel the emotions and energies of other people, animals, and objects through their body and their emotions. This ability to "feel" allows us to be highly sensitive and attuned to ourselves and others. There is this natural pull or desire to help others, help humanity, make a difference in someone's life. Clairsentients are natural healers due to their ability to be empathic. People feel completely understood and validated by them. They gravitate towards careers in which they are helping others, such as a counselor, teacher, coach, doctor, nurse, or therapist.

Clairalience means clear smelling.
This spiritual gift allows you to smell odors and fragrances that are not in your physical space. A common example would be smelling cigarette smoke, or the perfume or cologne of a deceased loved one to indicate their presence with us in this worldly realm. You may have a sensitivity to certain odors, like air fresheners, fragrances, or strong odors of any kind because of your heightened, strong sense of smell.

In 2019, my sister, daughter and I went on a trip to the Philippines. The housekeeper had washed our laundry and bedsheets. I was immediately overwhelmed by the strong scent of the laundry detergent when I laid my head on the pillow that night. So much so that it was making me cough and gag. I thought perhaps the laundry wasn't thoroughly rinsed in the wash cycle, or at all! I complained to everyone around me, yet no one else could smell anything. I was floored! How could they not smell that overpowering scent that was practically choking me? I felt burning in my airway through to my lungs.

Clairgustance means clear tasting.
This gift is the ability to taste a substance that is, again, not in your physical presence. It's more of an energetic taste. This could be a chemical, food, beverage or anything. It could be a stand-alone, random thing, or it could be attached to a person, place, or time. Perhaps a deceased loved one you associate it with (i.e. coffee or a cigarette after-taste). Just like with clear smelling, it is a way to communicate their presence near you. Other alterations you may experience: digestive changes, mouth-watering, dry mouth, hiccups, or needing to clear your throat.

One time, during an intuitive reading I was doing for someone, I sensed myself salivating, followed by having this bad taste and feeling nauseous. I was describing the symptoms to her, and I could tell from the look on her face she was both surprised and uncomfortable. It immediately occurred to me that this person was suffering from an eating disorder, and this was Spirit's way of communicating this to me in order to help her.

Claircognizance means clear knowing.
This is otherwise known as Extrasensory perception (**ESP**). This is perception that occurs independently of the known sensory processes. So, you don't need to feel, hear, see, taste, or sense anything. You know it without logic, proof or evidence. It is an impression that God/Spirit impresses upon you, and you simply know it as truth. An example of this may be a premonition of something to come or knowing the truth about a situation or person you've never met. You know when people are lying to you. None of the other senses are involved. You just have an intense gut feeling and use that to guide you.

Do you think you know which one of the Clairs might be your dominant one based on the examples? If you're still not sure, here's an exercise you can try:

Find yourself a private, comfortable space to sit for a few minutes without distraction. It's best to do this outdoors somewhere if possible, even in your own backyard. Start by just being an observer of your surroundings, taking in all details and feelings of where you are. Just sit with that for a bit and take it all in. Now, close your eyes and focus on your breath as if you were meditating—deeply, slowly, fully. In your mind's eye, do a mental replay of what you observed and noticed most just a few minutes earlier. Was it the sounds of the birds and the swaying of the trees in the wind? Was it something you specifically saw that caught your eye like a butterfly? Or were you daydreaming or having visions about anything in particular, maybe a person? Was it the feeling of the sun shining down your face? Was it the smell of McDonald's down the street? Was it the taste in your mouth or anything related to your digestive system, like being hungry? Were you thinking audibly in your head about anything in particular? Did it have pictures, images, words?

If you weren't sure during this exercise, keep trying it. Do it both indoors and outdoors and at random times, wherever you are. You could be laying in bed, you could be a passenger in someone's car, you could be sitting at the doctor's office. Any time, any day, just bring some awareness around it. You will eventually sharpen whatever your dominant sense is, and maybe even the others as you intentionally engage all your senses:

Take an orange and hold it in front of you. Make sure you have a paper towel or plate as well on the table or floor in front of you. Take a good look at your orange. Turning it around to visibly see all parts of its skin. Really study every inch of it. Now, close your eyes and in your mind's eye, rewind that visual and play it over again in your mind. Think about how you held the orange in front of you, slowly started turning it around inch by inch. Magnify it in your mind as if you had a zoom lens and focus in deeper. What did you notice as you looked at it? Were there bruises, creases, yellowing, dents...NO peeking. Only use your mind's eye. Concentrate. Take your time and breathe. Relax while you're doing it. Now with your eyes still closed, smell the orange. Place it gently up against your nose. Take a gentle inhale. Pay attention to how the odor hits your nasal passageways. Is it comfortable? Is it too strong? Does the orange smell the same as you slowly turn it? Is the scent stronger in some areas? When you move it further out in front of you, can you still smell it? Are there other scents you are noticing besides the orange? Now, let's use our tactile senses. How does the orange feel in your hand? Is it the size of a softball, a tennis ball? Is it soft, is it hard—what is the texture? Is it smooth, rough, bumpy? Is it cold, warm, room temperature?

With your eyes still closed, go ahead and peel the orange using your thumb and hands. Feel the sensation of your thumb digging into the orange. Listen to the sound it makes as you peel it. Pay attention to the additional scents that may come from it. Is there juice dripping down your hands or is the orange dry? Peel off the stringy skin undercoating that covers it. What does that feel like on your fingers? Is it sticky, is it dry, is it soft, is it hard? Now, split the orange in half. Did more aroma come out of it? Did it slightly spray more juices on your fingers? Gently pull apart a piece and place it in your mouth. Was it wet or dry? How did it feel when it hit your tongue? Was there a taste—bitter, sweet? Now bite into it and feel and taste the juices squirt out into your mouth or the back of your throat. Really savor it. Don't rush it. Let it sit in your mouth for a few minutes as you notice the changes in texture and shape. Visualize it in your mouth and what it may look like as you continue to bite into it. Feel your saliva mixing in with it, preparing it for digestion. Can you still smell the orange in your nose? When you're ready to swallow, feel the sensation of it going down your throat, through your esophagus and into your stomach. Can you feel it in your stomach? Did your stomach react with a grumble or feeling? Is your stomach hungry for more? What's in your mind's eye visually? What senses are engaged right now? Do you still have awareness of the rest of the orange that is sitting in your hand? What does the rest of the orange feel like in your hand? You can continue on with this exercise or you can stop here.

That is an example of heightening our senses. Engaging them individually and then collectively to create the full experience. Have you ever spent so much time savoring an orange?! Feel free to do that with any fruit or food. We are so used to just shoving food into our mouths that we rarely experience all there is to eating something. It can be a whole experience!

You can also try to reflect back on this experience at a later time with your eyes closed and recreate it as if you were doing it in real-time. During that time, you can also gauge which of your senses was most prominent. Was it the ability to recall every visual detail of the orange and the whole experience itself? Or was it your mouth watering at recalling the events? Or could you smell the scents as if they were in front of you again? Just be curious at what you notice the second or third time you recall the experience, doing it in the same fashion, but just using your memory.

Also, consider characteristics or preferences you have that you may have never questioned and just thought: "That's just the way I am." Does it bother you when you are at a restaurant or movie theatre and the fan or A/C is blowing directly on you? Are your eyes sensitive to the sun or bright places? Do you prefer a dark ambience when dining out? Does being near the ocean or nature make you feel a certain way? How important are your surroundings in how you feel? Are you any particular way in your own home? Are you a clean freak? Do air fresheners or fragrances bother you? Do certain fabrics of clothing bother you? What type of sheets do you like in your bed? Do you care? Does it have to be soft or silky? What is the primary way you learn? What is your love language? Do you like receiving gifts because it makes you "feel" a certain way? Do you like to "hear" words of affirmation? Does spending quality time with someone energize you? Is your perfect date watching the sunset because of the beautiful scenery? Which of your senses bring about the most pleasurable experience for you? Which brings the worst? Again, all you want to do is bring more and more awareness around this. Get to know yourself in a whole new way. Take inventory. Be curious. Take a step outside of yourself and be an observer. It might be easier to think about it when you first get up in the morning and consider what your routines are. What does your day look like?

When it comes to your Clairs and opening up your intuitive channels, practice makes progress. Once you become more aware and crack that door open, a whole new world begins to slowly emerge and you'll see that God, the Universe, and Spirit have been talking to you all along. You just weren't dialed into the right frequency. There is one last piece to all this that ties it all together and it is what I call the sixth love language: synchronicity.

Notes

9

The Sixth Love Language: Synchronicity

The language of the Universe, although can be complex in interpreting, has every intention to reach you and be known by you. Synchronicity for someone on the spiritual path is that moment when you become consciously aware that you have made a deeper connection with the Universe. It is a very "Deja Vu" feeling. Although these messages may be random at first to get your attention, once they do, the messages and guidance you seek will be so specific to you. It will be a two-way communication. I believe God attempts to reach us and speak to us in different ways. After all, we are in this world, but not of this world. Being in this world requires us to have a physical body. That body was equipped with an energetic system to tune in to certain frequencies in this world. Within this physical, energetic body is a Spirit, a Soul, that wants to be at the forefront and not in the background. It wants to awaken you to a whole new experience in this world, this realm we are temporarily in. The language of the Universe/God is unlike any language you have spoken. It is abstract; it uses symbolism and signs. It uses synchronicities.

Synchronicities are "meaningful coincidences" that occur with no causal relationship, yet seem to be meaningfully related. The term was originally coined by psychologist Carl Jung in which he refers to it as meaningful (or even miraculous) coincidences that occur in your life. When you experience synchronicity, you'll have experiences that seem far too significant to be mere day-to-day serendipitous encounters. So, what does this look like?

Storytime

Let me take you back to my flight from Hawaii to Las Vegas from chapter six. Remember, I told you I would refer back to that experience in the later chapters? This is where it all ties together. As you might recall, that book "The Alchemist" was sitting on my nightstand for six months collecting dust. I decided to bring it on my six-hour flight from Hawaii to Vegas for the sole purpose of "helping time fly by". Instead, as I was in the weeds of the book, it made time stop!

This charming little masterpiece of a book was the story of Santiago:

...a shepherd boy, who yearns to travel in search of a worldly treasure as extravagant as any ever found. The story of the treasures Santiago finds along the

way teaches us, as only a few stories can, about the essential wisdom of listening to our hearts, learning to read the omens strewn along life's path, and, above all, following our dreams. (Coelho, 1993)

For most of us, reading or hearing the word "omen" has a negative and scary connotation. In fact, I recall a movie called, "The Omen", and that little boy scared me to death! I, like you, have only ever thought that omens were bad or evil things. Until I spoke to my Christian, metaphysical mentor about it, Dr. Michael Bressem. He wrote that article I referred to in chapter one about this very topic, entitled, "Divination and The Bible" (2011):

Further, the interpretation of signs was also used in scripture; "sign or signs" is mentioned over 150 times in the Bible. Signs are given as:

1) an omen of future events about to take place (e.g., Revelation 12: 1-3)
2) as confirmation of God's will or presence (e.g., Judges 6; 17-22; John 12:37)
3) as a reminder of God's covenant with His people (e.g., Genesis 9:12)

King David prayed for signs (Psalm 86:17) and when God spoke to King Ahaz, God told him to ask for a sign (Isaiah 7: 12). Therefore, it doesn't seem wrong for God's people to seek signs - even astrological ones (e.g., Luke 21:26) as did the Magi. (Matthew 2:2)

"Omens", in the context I use and believe in it, has prophetic significance. It is a delivered message from the supernatural world into our natural world. It comes in the form of signs and symbols that cannot be mistaken. It can signify change, confirmation of events in your life, indicate something good, serve as a warning, provide guidance and most importantly, feel God's presence in a way like never before.

So, there I was reading the words on the pages of this little book. As Santiago's journey unfolds, he sees these signs, "omens", along his journey to find a worldly treasure. Just as I was reading this, the stewardess walked by to do the drink and snack service. She reached over to hand me a bag of crackers and some potato chips. Normally I would decline because I'm always trying to watch my carb and processed food intake, but for some reason, I accepted it. I resumed my reading of Santiago's journey:

> In order to find the treasure, you will have to follow the omens. God has prepared a path for everyone to follow. You just have to read the omens that he left for you". Before the boy could reply, a butterfly appeared and fluttered between him and the old man. He remembered something his grandmother had once told him that butterflies were a good omen. Like crickets, and like grasshoppers; like lizards and four-leaf clovers. (Coelho, 1993)

With my eyes continuing to be peeled on the pages, I opened up the bag of crackers and pulled out this:

"In order to find the treasure, you will have to follow the omens. God has prepared a path for everyone to follow. You just have to read the omens that he left for you."

Before the boy could reply, a butterfly appeared and fluttered between him and the old man. He remembered something his grandfather had once told him: that butterflies were a good omen. Like crickets, and like grasshoppers; like lizards and four-leaf clovers.

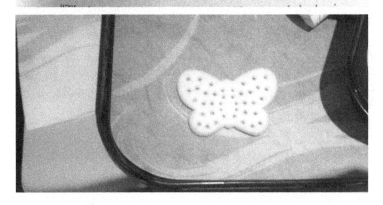

Oh. My. God! I quickly snapped a photo of it, as I had with many other synchronicities that had been happening in the two years prior. I later found out that butterflies were a powerful symbol of change and transformation. It deeply resonates with the Christian belief of ascension and endless potential transformation and spiritual rebirth. This had been my exact path during this time. I had gone through a painful divorce in 2012, then met that soul connection the day my divorce was finalized and inevitably went through another painful breakup the following year. I was going through some major, major healing. I was being transformed through the pain, forcing me to look inward and dig deep. I had been unbearably heartbroken for another full year thereafter. I was reading this book in the fall of 2014, and I was just healing from all the trauma, learning to love myself, learning to hold healthy boundaries, learning to put myself first, and never giving more than I was receiving in relationships.

My healing journey was my soul's cry out to God. I journaled and read scripture through my pain. I was attending retreats at church, which would be life-changing. I surrounded myself with loving, amazing friends and family. During that time, I was experiencing God's presence all around me in ways I never had before: through synchronicities on the time on the clock (11:11 a.m./p.m. and a series of repeating numbers, such as 1:11, 2:22, 3:33, 4:44, 5:55). Repeating numbers would show up on my store receipts, license plates, airline tickets, totals on my gas pump, the clock on my computer, my microwave—literally

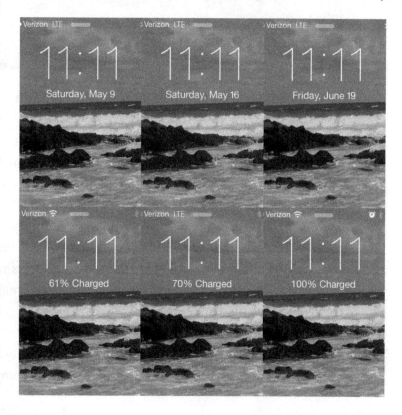

EVERYWHERE. I was bombarded with them. I would glance at something at just the right time, and it would stop me in my tracks. I definitely knew I wasn't going through this journey alone. I was spiritually awakening to a whole new world, to a whole new relationship with Him, and the Universe. I knew that everything I had suffered through in my journey wasn't in vain. There was a purpose. I made it through the painful metamorphosis...and out came the butterfly.

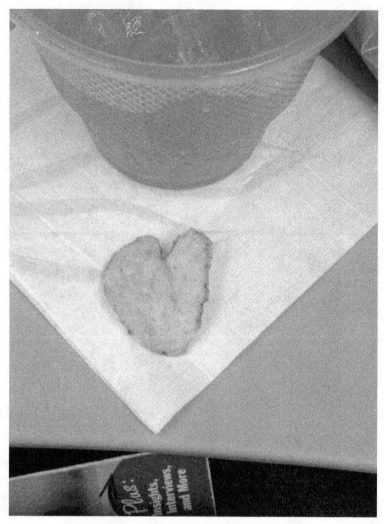

Many magical things happen in our lives. They happen every day, but we either don't see them because we aren't paying much attention and being fully present or we chalk it up to mere coincidence. I'm here to tell you, there are no coincidences—only synchronicities.

The story of the penny:

In 1998, I was pregnant with my daughter, Cassidy. We were stationed in Panama, Central America as her dad was in the Air Force. When you're pregnant, you see the doctor at regular intervals to track the pregnancy, and they conduct a series of prenatal exams, blood work, etc. to monitor the baby's health. One such test was something called the Triple Marker. The test analyzes how likely an unborn baby is to have birth/genetic/chromosomal defects (although they didn't inform me of this at the time). A simple blood test was drawn during my 16th week of pregnancy. I never gave it another thought, and home I went. A few days later, I received a call from the nurse asking me if I could come in to see the doctor that same day. Upon arrival, I was told by the doctor that my Triple Marker was positive, meaning it indicated that my baby could have Down's Syndrome; however, to be completely certain, she recommended I schedule an amniocentesis, which is a procedure where they insert this very long needle through your belly to extract some of the amniotic fluid that protects and surrounds the baby. This procedure carries a risk of infection as well as miscarriage. I was so scared, devastated, and in shock.

For the next several days, all I did was research as much as I could about this "Triple Marker test". Come to find out, it had a very high rate of false positives (hopefully they have improved this in the last 22 years!). This was not explained to me by the doctor and staff either. I had never been so stressed in my life. I had to make a decision fairly quickly as they made sure I knew, "Terminating the pregnancy would be best done sooner than later." The more I read about this inaccurate testing, the angrier I got.

I asked the doctor about another option I read about, which was just an ultrasound, basically. She stated that it was an option, but it wasn't 100% accurate in comparison to the amniocentesis because they would be relying strictly on the measurements of the baby, unless anything else was visibly blatant. After talking it over with my then husband and family, and after lots of anguish and prayer, we decided we would just do the ultrasound and not risk the baby. We had lots of sleepless and stressful nights leading up to the ultrasound.

The day finally arrived and we made our way to the waiting area of the hospital. It was later in the evening, and no one was around except the technicians in the back office. We sat there nervously waiting, seated across from each other. It was so quiet in the whole hospital. No one anywhere in sight. We decided to pray together while waiting. We leaned forward to hold hands as we bowed our heads to pray. We both started praying with our eyes closed, tears flowing down, when all of a sudden, out of nowhere, we hear what sounded like a coin drop from up above, land on the floor, bounce and roll near us.

The sound came from off to the side of us. We both immediately opened our eyes, wondering if someone had walked in the room and dropped some change. But when we opened our eyes, there was no one there. It was quiet and still, except for a single penny that landed right next to us. We stared at each other, picked it up, and rushed to the door to see if anyone was in the hallway. It was completely still. So quiet, you could hear a coin drop (sorry, I couldn't resist!). We sat back down and a few moments later, we were called back. I felt this sense of peace as I laid there during the ultrasound. I just knew everything was going to be O.K.

After the test, they told us they didn't see any concerns with the baby's measurements. Everything looked normal. Praise God! From that day forward, I had peace. It didn't matter what the doctors said. Needless to say, Cassidy Rae who is now 22, was a healthy baby girl! To this day, her dad carries around that penny in a special case in his wallet. The omen of the lucky penny!

There are no limitations in how Spirit can communicate with us. It's such a personal relationship, although there are some commonalities in people's experiences. Here's somewhat of a guideline you can use:

1) Repeating numbers in any order – They can be all the same like 222 or they can be in ascending or descending order, like 123 or 987. They can be any other significant numbers like birthdays, anniversaries, and that of deceased loved ones as well. Some believe that seeing numbers is how angels, specifically, communicate with us. Some like to refer to numerology to decode messages. Whatever resonates with you, do that.

2) White feathers – Signifying the presence of angels. Signifying the element of air. They may fall directly on your path, get stuck on your car windshield, or fall on your body from mid-air. However it shows up, you will know that it's not just some random thing. I often keep them if they happen to land on me or float right in front of my nose.

3) Repeated animal or insect sightings – These can be certain birds, dragonflies, butterflies, snakes, foxes, moths, and horses. It can be any animal or insect, and it can come in the form of dreams or just seeing it frequently in various ways, whether that be in a magazine, walking by a store, a sticker on someone's car, or somebody's tattoo you happen to glance at. You will continue to see it over, and over, and over again until you understand the message being relayed. The way to interpret the message is to understand the characteristics of that animal or insect. Remember, it's about symbolism. They serve as a messenger.

During my healing and transformation, I used to hear a very specific bird call every morning when I pulled up to work in my car. It was so loud and had such an unusual, distinct sound. It would stop me in my tracks because it was so persistent. I began to notice this bird from a distance, perched up at the highest point, whether that be on a building or a treetop. Once I noticed it, it would stop and fly away. This happened over and over. Then, it progressed to showing itself to me more closely. It would land on a tree right in front of me or in the parking stall. It was a bright red cardinal, not a bird I had seen much living in Oahu, Hawaii. Pretty soon, it was blatantly trying to be noticed by me: landing on my windowsill, swooshing directly over my windshield on the freeway, landing on a table I used to have lunch on, and even popping up on the other side of the island.

I finally had to look up the meaning of this persistent sighting. It was only then that I realized that cardinals were the most notable spiritual messengers from the spirit world for centuries. From a Christian context, red cardinals represent the blood of Jesus, representing life, vitality, hope, and restoration. They appear unexpectedly during difficult times to remind us to embrace new beginnings. Pretty soon, I began seeing this bird in other ways. For example, at my doctor's office in a painting on the wall. It had been there all along, and I never noticed it. Or at a random store I stopped in when I was out of town. I even heard it in a meditation where the background was nature sounds. It was truly amazing.

4) Through other people – People carry messages you need to hear at just the right time. They themselves may not realize they were led to you on that appointed date and time to hear exactly what you needed, but they were. It could be a stranger, a friend, a pastor's sermon, or a conversation you overhear at the store.

5) Through music/lyrics of songs – All of a sudden, you hear a song on the radio, while you're out at the store, or working, and the lyrics just seem like they're talking to you. You begin to hear the same song so frequently in random places: at a nail salon, blasting from a car next to you on the road, or in line at Starbucks. There's a strong connection you feel in that moment to those words.

6) Through your thoughts – All of a sudden, someone may pop into your mind and you feel compelled to check in with them. You then find out they're struggling through something and God nudged you to connect with them and provide encouragement and support.

7) Through words or pictures – The bumper or back of a car driving in front of you may have a sticker, a word, a phrase, or an image that speaks to you. The billboards you pass by. Social media posts that speak to you.

8) Other symbols from nature – Seeing a rainbow, a kite, a rock, the ocean, the Moon, flowers, a tree. Just keep your spiritual eyes open and pay attention to what you come into contact with.

Consider what keeps appearing and reappearing in your life and what you're drawn to.

9) Objects – You can come across an object that triggers a memory of a person, then you'll suddenly hear from them. Or if they're deceased, an overwhelming emotion will come over you because you feel their presence. Or when you lose something and ask for help finding it. Then suddenly, you're prompted to look at just the right random place where you wouldn't have otherwise thought to look. Objects can also fall or break. Objects can appear that are related to something that's been on your mind that you may be contemplating, and boom, there it is to nudge you towards that direction.

10) Through your dreams (or during meditation) – You can have premonitions of things to happen. You can have vivid dreams about people and places. You may get guidance from someone in the form of a dream. The symbols and signs can show up in your dreams. If you tend to have nightmares rather than dreams, that is because you likely have unhealed emotions and trauma trapped that are trying to come out for processing.

11) Technology malfunctions – Consider that when your connection to technology goes out and you have no service or it's acting up (Wi-Fi, internet, cell, TV) that perhaps it is forcing you to unplug, detach, and go within. We already discussed how we are now in a world of constant connection but to the wrong things.

12) Breakdowns to breakthroughs – Has your life ever completely turned upside down? It's one thing after another: you lose your job, your relationship ends, you got into a car accident, you have a death in the family, you lose your house—any series of events that just feel

like you've been pushed to the point of no return. These breakdowns can be opportunities to reevaluate things in our life, start over anew, make shifts, heal, and see things we need to change in our lives.

13) Roadblocks, detours and closed doors – Spirit's way of helping us along our journey and keeping us on the right path. *"Be thankful for closed doors, detours, and roadblocks. They protect you from paths and places not meant for you." – Suzanne Heyn*

Other things in the cosmos to consider that have spiritual components and influences:

Planetary influences:
Astronomy and astrology combined: RETROGRADES.

I never knew this until my sensitivities fully opened up, and I noticed during certain times (full moons and retrogrades) things would get stirred up inside and outside my life. It came in distinct cycles. Planetary cycles, that is. So, what is a retrograde? When the Earth completes its orbit around the Sun faster than the other planets outside its orbit and outpaces them, then retrograde occurs. Planets can't actually move backwards or retrograde in their orbit— they just "appear" to. It is an illusion. It's similar to when you're slowly pulling into a parking stall and the person in the stall next to you is backing out. At just the right vantage point, it feels like a weird optical illusion. Astrologists and their followers can attest that this planetary illusion actually has real effects on our lives.

Just as each planet appears to stop and move backwards on its cosmic path, we are being asked to do the same thing within our own lives. It's a time to press "pause" and review the trajectory we've been on. Retrogrades are periods of "RE"–reassess, reflect, redo, revisit, return, remove, and reevaluate. As is true for all things in nature, retrogrades happen in cycles, and it's different for each planet. Each planet has its own retrograde pattern. The most common and popular one being Mercury retrograde. This occurs about three to four times a year, and each of those periods lasts for about three weeks. That's pretty frequent compared to other planets, which is why this particular transit gets so much attention.

To better understand this, each planet in astrology rules over a different area of our lives (love, home, finances, career, etc.), and it's within those areas that we'll experience the retrograde effects, depending on which planet is in retrograde. For example, Mercury is the planet of communication and the mind. It affects our intellect, the way we think, learn, express ourselves, our perception and awareness. It is not uncommon at all for people's "stuff/baggage" to come up during a retrograde period because it "pulls us backward" to heal old wounds. Miscommunications happen in our relationships, which guides us to look within. If there's a relationship you had been hanging on to for too long, that's not serving your highest good, then the retrograde period may just help you finally move forward. Our perceptions are skewed during these retrogrades, so it is said not to make any big decisions during that time. It also affects transportation, contracts, and travel. It may seem really strange reading all this and a bit "woo-woo". I am not one to follow astrology much, especially not the horoscopes in the papers, but I will tell you from first-hand experience that we (in the physical, worldly realm) are affected by the things happening in the cosmos. I have an abundance of stories I could share in my own personal life of contract negotiations falling through, errors in contracts, flight changes and delays, break-ups happening, miscommunication in all relationships due to perceptions and perspectives being skewed and emotions running high, and especially my tech issues. Every single time my computer would have issues and crash. My phone would do some very odd things. Even people who work in the tech industry (IT support) who do not follow astrology and have no clue of what's happening in the cosmos, would say, "I don't know what's in the air, but we are slammed with people having tech issues the past few weeks now!" Umm, I know what's happening in the air, sir! It seems a bit strange for the average person to think this could be true, but when you think about it, why wouldn't it be? Everything is energy. We are reacting to energy. Think of retrogrades as a passing cloud of confusion over your life, meant for you to ponder, question, rethink and reevaluate. No action should be taken during that time. Just pause and do all the "REs". Once the cloud passes, there's clarity in the skies to move forward.

The Moon:
If the Moon can affect the ocean's tides by its gravitational pull and give rise to tides, what makes us think our human self isn't affected by the Moon as well, especially full Moons, being we are 60% water ourselves.

The infamous full Moon. It is used in scary movies and werewolf tales about the effects of the Moon on our human psyche. The word lunatic or lunacy is derived from the word LUNAR, which of course is how we refer to the Moon in the lunar calendar. So, is the mysterious full Moon really "crazy-making"? From a mystical perspective, the Moon represents powerful feminine energy, the feminine aspect of divinity. It signifies wisdom, intuition, birth, death, and reincarnation. In astrology:

...your moon sign is one of the most significant aspects of your astrological profile and is calculated based on the

position of the moon at your time of birth and represents your emotional inner world. The moon sign works behind the scenes, but it has a substantial impact on your character. It governs the steady ebb and flow of your moods; simply put, it's the internal "you". (Faragher, 2018)

The Moon's eight lunar phases happen because it orbits Earth. It's not actually the shape of the Moon that changes, only our perspective. The shape of the Moon changes because of the direction the sunlight is hitting it, which causes the portion we see illuminated to change.

There are eight lunar phases the Moon goes through in a 29.5-day lunar cycle, but the ones that are given the most attention are the new Moon and the full Moon (although each phase is known to have its own spiritual meaning). We can liken the whole 29.5-day cycle to a seed starting to grow and later on dying for another new beginning.

New Moon
In this phase, the Moon is between Earth and the Sun and is not visible on Earth. The darkness denotes the beginning, an instinct for birthing. As an example, think of a seed beneath the ground, representing the start of something new. At this phase, the energy builds in strength and intensity. It is the ideal time for you to set clear intentions and goals, start new projects or new ideas. The energy is greatly expanded when you create a ceremony (journal writing, lighting candles, or personal meditation), stating your desires and feeling them in your heart. The intention you set is fully supported by the lunar energy to come to completion by the full Moon in approximately 30 days. Of course, there are many phases in between the new and full Moon, to continue your intentions, but we will just focus on those two to keep it simple.

Full Moon

At this phase, the Moon, Earth, and Sun are aligned again just like the new Moon, but the Moon is on the other side of the Earth, directly opposite the Sun. Thus, the entire illuminated portion can be seen on Earth, full and round. The seed is in full bloom. This represents fertility, transformation, completion, and abundance. You can bask outside in the full Moon's energy, and it is very powerful. Just know there's also another side to the full Moon in that it can bring about stronger emotions, tension, and illuminate things in our life that need our attention (the healing aspect of the full Moon). It can also stir up some stuff that can rattle emotions, thus the term "lunatic". Just as the Moon can be cleansing to us and affect our energy, you can also use it to cleanse and charge your crystals if that is something you also use in your spiritual toolbox.

As you become more attuned and open, which are key in your ability to intuitively interpret the language and energy around you, then your gifts become more heightened and you can see things more abstractly. There are so many signs and symbols all around. Some call it winks from the Universe. It's all there to get your attention and show you support on your spiritual journey. It is truly a Divine experience.

There is a part of the world that we can't see, a realm of reality that doesn't consist of material things but of non-material forms. These forms are real even though they are invisible, because they have the potential to appear in our mind and act in it. – Carl Jung

147

A sampling of my camera roll, and so much more where this came from:

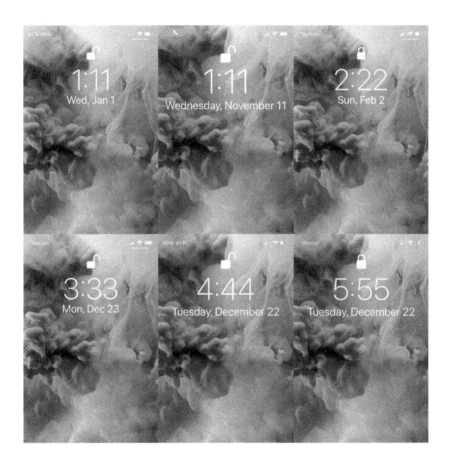

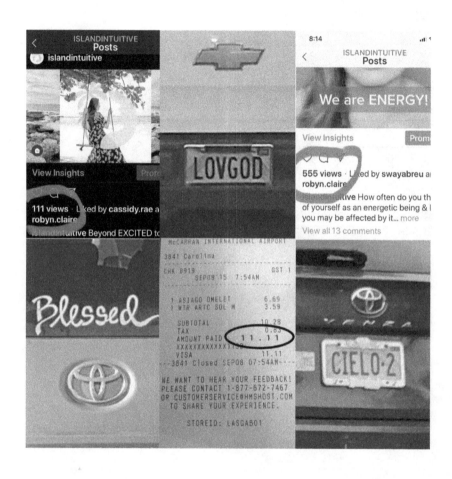

THE ALCHEMIST

"That's the principle that governs all things," he said. "In alchemy, it's called the Soul of the World. When you want something with all your heart, that's when you are closest to the Soul of the World. It's always a positive force."

"When you want something, all the universe conspires to help you achieve it," the old king had said.

"Synchronicity is an ever-present reality for those who have eyes to see." – Carl Jung

Notes

Intuition Unlocked!

Congratulations! You have now unlocked your intuition. You have and own the key! This is just the beginning. We have unlocked it and now you have the opportunity to unleash it in a big way that changes your life forever. It is powerful to experience that you are not walking this journey called "life" alone. You will have your own personal observations, revelations, and Divine guidance to help you gain powerful insight that will be different from anyone else, yet you will also experience commonalities. Thank goodness for that or I would have been so confused, lost, scared, and questioning what I was seeing or questioning if I was going crazy when I was going through this initially. I didn't have a point of reference, so Google was my best friend for three years. I was stunned that what I was experiencing was a phenomenon very well known in the spiritual community, and since at least 1960, when Swiss Psychologist Carl Jung wrote a book about it.

This intuitive journey is about rediscovering your soul. I believe that we are all here, as physical beings, to learn life lessons, grow, evolve, and be guided to return to our authentic selves. Like that GPS or Google Maps we spoke about in chapter one, you don't have to feel lost, alone, or be a mere observer of your life. You are a co-creator and participator of your reality. Life is not happening to you. It is happening with you and for you. There is guidance leading you to your life's purpose, to your path of abundance, to your dreams of success, to reaching and exceeding your goals, to the love you desire, and to the life you were meant to live.

Remember that the ego will always want and try to make logical sense of everything in your life. Human nature seeks very black and white answers to our problems: yes or no, this way or that way, up or down, left or right. Sometimes going down a different, unknown path is part of your lesson and journey. There are some things we can make sense of, and other things our limited human form will never be capable of understanding. His ways are far greater than our ways.

Be kind to yourself on life's journey and realize this IS a journey. But you never walk alone. You have the guidance all around you and all the answers within. Know and trust that truth. All you have to do is receive and believe.

Let's tie this journey up with a big, red bow, shall we?

You have a Superpower – Your intuition.

You have an Imposter –Your subconscious.

You have an ego – Your reactive voice!

You have a busy mind – That is trainable.

Intuition Unlocked!

You have a logical AND creative mind – Use both!

You have a soul – Nope, you ARE a soul. You have a body!

You have senses – Don't limit yourself to five.

You have the gift of Clairs – Discover which one(s)!

You have synchronicity – Use your Spiritual eyes!

You have intuition – It's unlocked!

Notes

About the Author

Cielo Canlas is a spiritual advisor, teacher, mentor, certified life coach, intuitive empath, and certified energy healing practitioner. She is known as the "Island Intuitive" on the beautiful island of Oahu, Hawaii, where she has run her own business and practice, of the same name, for the past three years. She is blessed with the gift of clairvoyance (clear-seeing), clairaudience (clear-hearing), clairsentience (clear-sensing or feeling), claircognizance (clear-knowing) and channeling (transmission of Divine healing energy). Her work has quickly reached clients from all over the world, who have benefitted greatly from her gifts and experienced life-changing shifts, guidance, and healing.

Cielo holds both traditional and non-secular credentials, including:

Master of Arts - Management/Psychology, Bachelor of Science - Human Services/Medical Studies, Bachelor in Metaphysical Science, Certified Professional Life Coach, Ordained Metaphysical Minister, and Certified Energy Medicine Practitioner. Cielo continues to work towards her Doctoral degree, expanding her knowledge and elevating the work that she does.

She has been interviewed as a guest on multiple podcasts and radio stations and has taught numerous workshops in all areas of spirituality, especially intuition. In addition to writing this book, Cielo was inspired to create her very own signature Intuitive Guidance cards for those wanting to explore, develop, and master their own intuitive gifts, or for those who simply want to receive Divine guidance on their life's journey.

Acknowledgements

There have been many instrumental people in my journey that I would like to acknowledge and thank. First and foremost, Dr. Michael Bressam, who mentored me and nurtured my spiritual gifts. He was with me during my darkest years, providing me with counsel and support, and I cannot thank him enough for that. He was a huge part of my healing journey. He knew me in my brokenness; a person no one would recognize today.

I would like to thank my soul family. Those who were brought into my life for seasons, reasons, and lifetimes. Gloria, my dearest friend and confidant, who I spend hours and hours talking spirituality with. She has heard all the stories, experienced the good, bad and ugly with me. She has helped pick up the pieces for me and my daughter, and I will always be thankful for her unwavering love and support. A journey of a thousand miles requires a soul companion, and she has been mine. I love you. A big thank you to all my other girlfriends who have loved me, cried with me, talked some sense into me, and pigged out with me. You are all amazing!

I want to say thank you to my exes, who shall remain nameless. You have served as my mirrors, my lessons, my quizzes, and my tests. You didn't make it easy to pass on to the 'next grade', but I wouldn't change a thing. The pain and suffering we endured together were a direct influence on my growth and wisdom. Thank you for doing the spiritual dance with me. I appreciate you, and I am glad we can remain friends to this day. You taught me how to love myself—what an invaluable gift!

To my dearest Paul, the talented photographer behind the infamous swing photo that beautifully covers this book. He's not only my photographer but also my videographer, producer and editor for my courses. He wears many different hats in helping me grow my business and practice, but most importantly, he is the one who has truly done the inner work with me. While my exes taught me how to love myself, Paul taught me how to love, period...in the truest sense of the word. Not superficial romanticized love, but real love—authentic, raw, and vulnerable, stripped of unconscious wounding and subconscious programming. It is rare. It is beautiful. It is healthy. It is conscious. We did it! I love you, and I love you even more for having loved me through it all, especially when I was not so lovable.

Free Guided Meditation

Download your FREE "Guided Sensory Meditation" audio file from Cielo's website: https://www.islandintuitive.com/free-meditation-downloads

Using guided imagery, Cielo takes you on a relaxing journey through an orchard filled with oranges. Each step of the way, her vivid words will engage your active imagination, bringing a new-found presence and awareness to your mind, body, senses, and beyond.

Follow Island Intuitive on social media:

https://www.instagram.com/islandintuitive/

https://www.facebook.com/islandintuitive/

https://www.tiktok.com/@islandintuitive?

Free Facebook group for Sensitive Souls:

https://www.facebook.com/groups/sensitivesoulsgroup

CONTACT INFO:

(808) 824-1141
info@islandintuitive.com
www.islandintuitive.com

Island Intuitive
"She is SPOT on!"

►Work with Cielo:

Work with Cielo, Island Intuitive, one-on-one. Visit her website www.islandintuitive.com to browse through her services and book an appointment. She is available remotely via Zoom, Skype or Facetime, so there are no geographical boundaries in experiencing her amazing work and energy. She is infamously known for being "spot on!" View her clients' 5-star reviews under the "Testimonials" tab of her website.

►Learn from Cielo:
https://www.islandintuitive.com/courses

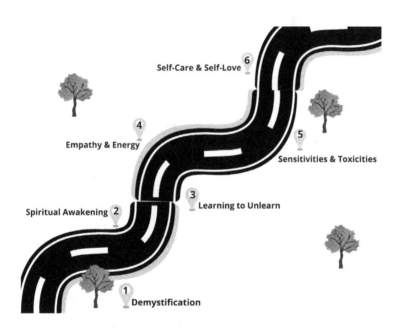

Are you an empath or highly sensitive person (HSP) yourself? Sign-up for Cielo's online course, "Foundations of Being a Sensitive Soul." These six modules will help you navigate your sensitive nature and

THRIVE, not just survive! It is the course you knew you needed with the transformation you never expected!

Cielo has walked this path before you and created this roadmap, so you don't ever have to feel lost or alone.

▶Intuit with Cielo:

https://www.islandintuitive.com/intuitive-guidance-cards

Catapult your intuition by using Cielo's very own Intuitive Guidance cards.

Each watercolor image, quote, and message on this 75-card deck was Divinely inspired to her by God. Use your own intuition to interpret the images and receive specific messages through your Higher Self and/or use the accompanying guide, which provides profound wisdom to support you on your journey.

Cielo C. Canlas

Island Intuitive
"She is SPOT on!"

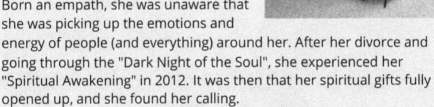

Cielo Canlas is known as "Island Intuitive" and lives in the beautiful island of Oahu, Hawaii. She is the author of "Intuition Unlocked. Discover your Superpower. Speak the Language of the Universe". Born an empath, she was unaware that she was picking up the emotions and energy of people (and everything) around her. After her divorce and going through the "Dark Night of the Soul", she experienced her "Spiritual Awakening" in 2012. It was then that her spiritual gifts fully opened up, and she found her calling.

She is now a spiritual advisor, teacher, minister, coach, mentor, healer and speaker. She teaches courses and workshops on intuition, being an empath or highly sensitive person, the spiritual awakening process and all things in the spiritual realm. She has clients worldwide who have sought her expertise through their own spiritual journey. Cielo has guested on multiple podcasts, radio stations, and has spoken in various metaphysical expos and schools. She feels extremely blessed to share her wisdom, gifts, and light with the world.

 @islandintuitive  www.islandintuitive.com   info@islandintuitive.com   islandintuitive

References

Chapter 1:

Bressam, M. (2011). *Divination and the Bible*

Dictionary.com. (2021). Psychic. In *Dictionary.com* website. Retrieved March 1, 2021, from https://www.dictionary.com/browse/psychic

Merriam-webster. (n.d.). Psychic. In *Merriam-Webster.com dictionary*. Retrieved March 1, 2021, from https://www.merriam-webster.com/dictionary/psychic

Northrop, C. (2020). *Women's Bodies, Women's Wisdom: Creating Physical and Emotional Health and Healing*. Hayhouse.

Wikipedia. (2021). Psychic. In *Wikipedia.com* website. Retrieved on March 1, 2021, from https://en.wikipedia.org/wiki/Psychic

Chapter 2:

Atman, T. (Host). (2020 Feb 26). *LegGO of my EGgO*. The Stuck Stops Here podcast.

Barbash, E. (2017). *Different Types of Trauma: Small 't' versus Large 'T'*. PsychologyToday.com

Fannin & Williams (n.d.). *What Neuroscience Reveals about the Nature of Business*. https://www.marietteham.org/uploads/5/0/9/6/50963181/fannin_ea._mind-brain_interface_what_neuroscience_reveals_about_the_nature_of_business.pdf

Chapter 3:

Eckhart, T. (2008). *A New Earth.* https://www.sloww.co/eckhart-tolle-a-new-earth-101/#ANEego

LePera, N. @Holistic Psychologist. (2021 Feb 23). *How to do ego work.* https://www.instagram.com/p/CLqUq7OgZif/?utm_source=ig_web_copy_link

Lipton, B. (2019). *Taking Back Our Power.* https://upliftconnect.com/dr-bruce-lipton-taking-back-our-power/

Orloff, J. (2018). *The Empath's Survival Guide: Life Strategies for Sensitive People.*

Paul, M. (2020). *What Emotional Triggers Are + Why You Need To Understand Them.* https://www.mindbodygreen.com/0-18348/what-are-emotional-triggers-why-you-need-to-understand-them.html

What is the function of the various brainwaves? (1997). https://www.scientificamerican.com/article/what-is-the-function-of-t-1997-12-22/

What is NLP? (2021). https://www.nlp.com/what-is-nlp/

Chapter 4:

Davidson & Lutz. (2009). *Buddha's Brain: Neuroplasticity and Meditation.* National Institute of Health. https://www.ncbi.nlm.nih.gov/pmc/articles/PMC2944261/

Fletcher, E. (2021). *The M word Meditation.* https://www.mindvalley.com/mword

Goldstein, E. (2011). *Cognitive Psychology* (Third ed., pp. 24-76). N.p.: Linda Schreiber-Ganster.

Liou, S. (2016). Neuroplasticity. In web.stanford.edu. Retrieved February 9, 2021, from https://hopes.stanford.edu/neuroplasticity/

Powell, A. (2018). *When science meets mindfulness.* The Harvard Gazette. https://news.harvard.edu/gazette/story/2018/04/harvard-researchers-study-how-mindfulness-may-change-the-brain-in-depressed-patients/

Seshadri, N. (2019). *What is Intuition.* https://mindandsoul.space/home/2019/9/1/what-is-intuition

Tassell, D. V. (2004). *Neural Pathway Development.* In www.brains.org. Retrieved September 9, 2016, from http://www.brains.org/path.htm

References

Chapter 5:

Fletcher, E. (2005). *Balancing Breath - Ziva Meditation.* https://www.youtube.com/watch?v=wHc-fjonnek&t=206s

Horowitz, N. (1997). Roger W. Sperry. https://www.nobelprize.org/prizes/medicine/1981/sperry/article/

Kurth & Graham. (2015). *Shifting brain asymmetry the link between meditation and structural lateralization.* https://pubmed.ncbi.nlm.nih.gov/22374478/

Luders & Phillips et al. (2012). *Bridging the hemispheres in meditation.* https://pubmed.ncbi.nlm.nih.gov/22374478/

Pietrangelo, A. (2019). *Left Brain vs. Right Brain: What Does This Mean for Me?* https://www.healthline.com/health/left-brain-vs-right-brain

Reed & Gramly. (2021). *A Beginner's Guide to Pranayama.* Yoga Journal. https://www.yogajournal.com/practice/beginners/how-to/pranayama/

Shmerling, R. (2017). *Right brain/left brain, right?* https://www.health.harvard.edu/blog/right-brainleft-brain-right-2017082512222

Chapter 6:

LePera, N. @HolisticPsychologist (2020). https://www.instagram.com/the.holistic.psychologist/

Wyatt, K. (2015). *The Butterfly Principle: Transformation and Growth Through Failure.* https://www.huffpost.com/entry/the-butterfly-principle-transformation-and-growth-through-failure_b_7992790

Chapter 7:

American Cancer Society (2020). Article on *Radiofrequency (RF) Radiation.* https://www.cancer.org/cancer/cancer-causes/radiation-exposure/radiofrequency-radiation.html#references

Guzman, I. (2017). *Tuning in to the Earth's Natural Rhythm.* https://brainworldmagazine.com/tuning-in-to-the-earths-natural-rhythm/

Marzvanyan & Alhawai. (2020). *Physiology, Sensory Receptors.* https://www.ncbi.nlm.nih.gov/books/NBK539861/

Wang & Hilburn. (2019). *Transduction of the Geomagnetic Field as Evidenced from alpha-Band Activity in the Human Brain.* https://www.eneuro.org/content/6/2/ENEURO.0483-18.2019

Smith, L. (2019). *What are binaural beats, and how do they work?* https://www.medicalnewstoday.com/articles/320019

Tang & Yeh. (2019). *Effects of extremely low-frequency electromagnetic fields on B16F10 cancer cells.* https://pubmed.ncbi.nlm.nih.gov/30889982/

Chapter 8:

Rosen, R. (2010). *Developing your 5 clair senses.* https://www.oprah.com/spirit/developing-your-5-clair-senses-rebecca-rosen/all

Ross, C. (2009). *HUMAN ENERGY FIELDS: A New Science and Medicine.* http://www.rossenergysystems.com/Downloads/Human-Energy-Fields-Intro.pdf

Chapter 9:

Coelho, P. (1993). Amazon excerpt: https://www.amazon.com/Alchemist-Paulo-Coelho/dp/0061122416

Faragher, A. (2018). *What Your Moon Sign Reveals About Your Emotional Personality.* https://www.allure.com/story/zodiac-moon-sign-emotional-personality

Ponte & Schafer. (2013). *Carl Gustav Jung, Quantum Physics and the Spiritual Mind: A Mystical Vision of the Twenty-First Century.* https://www.ncbi.nlm.nih.gov/pmc/articles/PMC4217602/

Notes

Notes

Notes

CPSIA information can be obtained
at www.ICGtesting.com
Printed in the USA
LVHW020349290921
698990LV00002B/170

9 781922 597311